YOUR PLAN IS

YOUR PARACHUTE

YOUR PLAN IS

YOUR PARACHUTE

SECOND EDITION

A SIMPLIFIED GUIDE TO
BUSINESS CONTINUITY
AND CRISIS MANAGEMENT

by

Jacques R. Island

Quest Publishing ❖ *Miami, Florida*

Inquiries should be directed to :

Quest Publishing
2655 S. Le Jeune Road, Suite 500
Coral Gables, FL 33134 U.S.A.
Tel. +1 305.779.3069 • Fax +1 305.901.2120
email: editor@quest-publishing.com

ISBN: 978-0-9769416-0-6
Library of Congress Control Number 2017963676

Editor: Elisabeth Mason

Second Edition: September 2019

10 9 8 7 6 5 4 3 2 1

Information in this book is distributed "as is" without warranty. It is sold with the understanding that it is intended only as a self-help guide and not as a substitute for legal, accounting or other professional services. Neither the author nor the publisher shall have any liability with respect to informa-tion contained herein. Further, neither the author nor the publisher have any control over or assume any responsibility for websites or external resources referenced in this book. While the author believes everything herein is accu-rate, any questions regarding specific situations should be addressed by appropriate professionals.

The blank forms in the back of this book may be reproduced for personal use. They are also available as large, letter-size (8.5"x11") blank forms from www.quest-publishing.com.

To my wife, Yvonne, whose considerable
organizational and legal skills keep
our company low-risk and sane;
and to my young daughter, Kamila,
who happily provides me with
opportunities for practicing
"crisis management" at home.

Contents

PART I   FUNDAMENTALS   1

PART II   THE PROCESS   57

List of Figures

List of Exercises

List of Tables

About the Author

Jacques Island has spent most of his working life with various U.S. Government agencies dealing with crises. After military service in Vietnam and Germany he was recruited into the U.S. Foreign Service as a counterintelligence/counter-terrorism agent-operative protecting U.S. embassies, dignitaries and diplomats on missions around the world, and foreign dignitaries on state visits to the U.S.

Crisis managers pride themselves as much for the crises they avert through good risk management as for the crises they successfully negotiate. Jacques is no exception.

Among the many potential and actual crises Jacques worked on during his many years with the U.S. Foreign Service was the evacuation of U.S. Embassy diplomats and citizens in Nicaragua during the height of that country's civil war. He was awarded a U.S. Department of State Meritorious Honor Service medal for his role in organizing and executing the ground and air evacuation from Nicaragua amidst chaotic fighting.

Crisis management was also a large part of Jacques' work during his 20-year career as an agent of the Federal Bureau of Investigation. During his tenure with the F.B.I. he worked major frauds, product tampering and piracy crimes that affected the solvency of victim companies, and dealt with prison uprisings, aircraft hijackings, hostage takings, and terrorists from the left, the right and from abroad that threatened the interests of the United States. He was trained and certified by the F.B.I. as a crisis negotiator and spent most of his F.B.I. career on their crisis management teams.

Upon retirement from the F.B.I. in 2002, Jacques turned his attention to the private sector as a RISC™ consultant to companies, large and small. This book is one more step in his efforts to help businesses reach greater crisis management awareness and preparation before they are hit by a ruinous event.

Preface

Businesses today are operating in an increasingly complex, litigious, and dangerous environment. In addition to the eternal calamities that could befall an enterprise—fire, war, crime, strife or natural disasters—now malevolent rivals can also interrupt or disable your business remotely and from relative safety.

To assure that our communities' businesses can prevail through trying times, Ms. Lettie Bien, the then President and CEO of the Coral Gables Chamber of Commerce, was the catalyst that, prior to her military deployment for duty in Iraq, established the Emergency Management Committee (EMC) to help businesses help themselves in crises. Then fresh out of the F.B.I. and my company (Inquesta) a new member of the Chamber, she asked me to chair the Committee.

The Committee's mission was to educate the business community on ways to avoid emergencies, to mitigate damage and revenue losses, and to accelerate their recovery from a crisis.

The idea of producing a new book was sparked when I was also asked to produce business continuity planning (BCP) workshops for South Florida and Chamber businesses. A search for BCP literature suitable for small businesses was found lacking, and I had to create original BCP training materials.

Those materials were then organized into what became the first (2004) edition of this book, titled *Business Continuity Planning: Preparing for the Inevitable Crisis,* to guide groups of small businesses in producing their own draft BCP during an eight-hour workshop.

Additional information has been added since that first edition to provide self-doers new to business continuity and crisis management with a better understanding of the process and better tools for producing their own business continuity plan quickly.

Inquesta's new book became useful for our company's consulting work and workshops for clients outside the U.S. as well.

Although the public services and regional infrastructures in various parts of the world differ (so strategies and responses to crises will need to be adapted to local realities), the methods and principles given here are applicable anywhere. The business continuity planner can adapt them to their particular region and business.

This book is intended to make crisis management relatively effortless, performed in a minimum of time with straight-forward, step-by-step guidance. It can be used as a self-help tool or as part of a workshop. Eight-hour workshops are recommended to accelerate the process even more through an interactive group effort, and to provide a venue for businesses seeking partners for their crisis recovery arrangements. Those charged with business continuity management for their firms can certainly create their own plan in a day's time using this book.

This second edition includes three case studies to jump start your company's plan. Each case study has accompanying completed worksheets and a resulting sample business continuity plan (BCP).

You can download digitial versions of the examples and empty worksheet templates from the publisher's website (quest-publishing.com). Simply choose which of the three cases most typifies your circumstances, then modify a template to fit your situation. Or, combine the elements of two or more.

You will note that this book is neither the shortest checklist variety of publication on this subject nor a long treatise on business continuity management. I have used many short to long references on this topic. I find that short checklists fail to explain adequately why and how you would prepare a business continuity plan. On the other hand, I don't know anyone who would pick up a book on this topic for pure reading pleasure, and less so if its explanations are esoteric.

Many books on crisis management are simply inspirational, or they just expound a new theory or process. They are fine, legitimate reading but, if they lack the methods and tools to cobble together a functional business continuity plan, they will not meet the practitioner's needs.

In writing this book I wanted to avoid producing a cryptic checklist or an encyclopedic dissertation. Hopefully you will agree that this book is a balance between those two extremes, and that it presents a simple methodology suitable for the uninitiated in business continuity management.

I am confident that you will find this book useful whether you choose to use it to create a business continuity program independently or in conjunction with a RISC™ management workshop.

Jacques R. Island
Miami, Florida
September, 2019

Acknowledgments

The author's gratitude goes to the many members of the Greater Miami Chamber of Commerce and the Coral Gables, Florida Chamber of Commerce's Emergency Management Committee (EMC) and participating businesses for their advice and suggestions while creating the first edition then titled *Business Continuity Planning: Preparing for the Inevitable Crisis*, first published in 2004, the foundation of this book.

Also noteworthy has been the significant energy that my able assistant, Eva Chovancova, spent helping me research and organize this book.

I

FUNDAMENTALS

This section introduces the topic of Business Continuity Management and provides a primer so the process section that follows—the creation of the actual plan's components—will make better sense.

CHAPTER

1

HOW RESILIENT IS YOUR BUSINESS?

There are no secrets to success.
It is the result of preparation, hard work,
and learning from failure.

— Colin Powell

WAVES OF FRANTIC people rushed through the long-emptied lumber and food markets at the eleventh hour in the Summer of 2005. Many others heeded the New Orleans' mayor's orders to evacuate inland to higher ground as Hurricane Katrina aimed at "The Big Easy."

But trying to move through roadways chocked with thousands of frantic drivers was easier said than done. And, with a 400-mile wide weather monster at their backs, once outside of the most dangerous part of the storm there was, still, a storm and no shelter from howling winds and rain.

New Orleans, a below-sea-level city in the delta of the mighty Mississippi, had kept the river banks at bay with levees constructed by the U.S. Army Corps of Engineers a century before. But the aging levees caused worry. Countless engineers and scientists had warned through the years of potential levee and dam failures.

The danger of living on a river delta has been on the minds of New Orleanians since the city was founded in 1718, but they trusted their ingenuity and levees, and they hoped the very slim chance of a direct hit by a major storm would not happen.

So it was that the much needed costly repairs to the area's levies were always put off for another day in lieu of other more immediate community needs.

And then the improbable happened.

This hurricane was not the most violent as hurricanes go but what the winds didn't wreck flood waters did. The storm's heavy rains filled the lakes and marshes until weak levees gave way and submerged 80% of the city.

Katrina killed almost 2,000 people.

SO MUCH CAN AND DOES GO WRONG

U.S. fires and storms that followed Katrina have caused even more deaths and destruction. For example, Hurricane Sandy affected the East Coast in 2012, including New York and New Jersey, caused $75 billion in damages and cost 147 lives; Hurricane Harvey in 2017 killed 107 and caused $125 billion in damages to Texas, Louisiana and Alabama; Hurricane Maria's ferocious category five winds stripped Puerto Rico of its trees, houses and infrastructure in 2017, left the island without power for nearly a year, killed nearly 6,000, and caused about $100 billion in damages; and California's wildfires since 2018 have killed at least 88 and have burned over $16 billion in property.

These are examples of U.S. natural disasters that normally give you hours if not days of notice. Given modern warning systems and communications, there may well be a lot you can do to "weather" a known, looming crisis.

Now imagine you are seated in your office concentrating on an urgent project when the floor beneath you suddenly and violently convulses and your papers are tossed off your desk by a heaving earth. You hear the straining pipes as walls and ceilings crack and you smell pulverized cement and plaster along with… what?…Gas!

You only have *seconds* to do the right thing provided you anticipated such an event in the first place. Unlike a hurricane, an earthquake gives practically no warning.

Will you be able to run outside quickly enough or know where inside you'll have the best chance of survival?

What if you are visiting a client's office on the 37th floor when the building begins a dizzying back and forth sway that topples books off the shelves? Or the fire alarms go off as you sense smoke? Did your host prepare for this?

Sudden disasters that give only moments to react can be, among others, a building fire, a failing structure like a bridge, an earthquake or a tsunami.

The 2004 Indian Ocean tsunami that originated off the coast of Sumatra killed 228,000 people! Many of the victims were

---

"Even if [a crisis] does not visit you early on, take heart in knowing that the time you spent preparing for the worst is not wasted; your business continuity preparations are also opportunities to fine-tune your truly essential business precesses, and identify company fat you can shed."

---

foreign vacationers in Thailand, Indonesia and other nearby countries. More recent tsunamis have occurred in Japan, Chile, the Solomon Islands, British Colombia (Canada), Samoa, Sumatra, New Zealand, and Iceland.

Coastal cities and low landmasses, like the Florida peninsula, are at increasing risk of going underwater as a result of a storm surge or a tsunami.

So far we've talked only about natural disasters. What about unnatural ones? The ones we humans cause by accident or design? There are plenty of those to consider for your plan.

In fact, businesses are as likely to face a crisis of the man-made kind: a deranged or vengeful gunman who sprays gunfire throughout your school, house of prayer, or workplace, or leaves a bomb in a shopping center or sports arena; an armed robbery that turns fatal to an employee or client; a disgruntled employee who sabotages your products and causes irreparable harm to people or your business.

School shootings are an example of what deranged young and not-so-young minds are capable of. These attacks are not new and they have become commonplace (almost monthly if not weekly) and increasingly deadly. Our children are no longer safe. They are now sought-after targets.

Terrorism also poses a larger threat with each passing year. The September 11th, 2001 destruction of New York's Twin Towers of the World Trade Center (9/11) heralded a plague of well-funded, trans-national, fanatically murderous extremist religious groups like al-Qaeda ("the Center") and ISIL ("Islamic State of Iraq and the Levant").

They may seem to be "defeated" but they are sure to rear up again before they finally do "die." As ISIL morphed out of a defeated al-Qaeda, so are ISIL's remnants reconstituting into a new threat. What was an "army" concentrated in Syria is metastasizing throughout Africa and Europe as small, dispersed cells.

The world can expect to face more fascist and extreme religious terrorists from all branches, from abroad or from homegrown groups, at least into the near future.

These groups and others carry out spectacular acts of terrorism through organized, coordinated attack cells and through sympathetic "lone wolves"—disaffected, self-radicalized people.

Entirely domestic extremist groups also cause tremendous destruction to life and property within a country's borders. The bombing of the Alfred Murrah Federal Building in Oklahoma City, Oklahoma in 1995 that killed 168 people and injured hundreds is an example of U.S. domestic terrorism.

A small sampling of other *domestic* terror attacks against U.S. businesses and non-profits since then that merit mention are—

- the anthrax poison letters mailed in 2001 to U.S. Congressmen in the Washington, D.C. area and to the National Inquirer (a publisher) in Florida that killed five persons and injured 17 was probably motivated by personal grudges held by the prime suspect, who committed suicide;

- two ISIS-inspired terrorists that set off bombs at the 2013 Boston Marathon killing four and injuring 280;

- a white supremacist who attacked a Charleston, South Carolina church with gunfire and killed nine people in 2015;

- a shooting attack at a Colorado Springs, Colorado Planned Parenthood clinic against its staff and patients in 2015 that resulted in three dead and nine wounded;

- two self-radicalized "Jihadists" who in 2015 attacked the San Bernardino, California (government) Regional Center with gunfire, and killed 14 and injured 22;

- a "Jihad"-inspired gunman who in 2016 attacked the Pulse nightclub, a gay locale in Florida, and killed 49 patrons and injured 53;

- the 2017 vehicle ramming attack in Charlottesville, Virginia during a neo-Nazi demonstration in which a neo-Nazi group member intentionally drove into counter demonstrators, and killed one and injured 28;

- another vehicle ramming in 2017 in New York City in which an ISIS-inspired terrorist drove a truck into cyclists, runners and pedestrians, and killed eight and injured 11;

- a terrorist who in 2018 posted anti-Semitic comments opposing Jewish support for Central American immigrants, then rampaged a Pittsburg synagogue with gunfire that killed 11 and injured 7;

- and the 2018 Stoneman Douglas High School attack in Parkland, Florida that killed 17 students and faculty and wounded 17 more.

This short list is but a smattering of the violence that is now commonplace in the U.S.

An example of domestic terrorism outside the U.S. is the Moscow Dubrovka Theater hostage crisis in the Russian Federation, in which about 40 Chechen separatists and 130 of the 850 hostages died in 2002.

A newer trend is for militants from the former Soviet Union's southern republics, who previously fought against their own repressive regimes at home, to focus increasingly on the international scene. Over 8,000 such militants flocked to Syria and Iraq during this decade to fight U.S. and NATO troops. We can expect this to continue and to expand their activities beyond the Middle East.

Figure 1.1: Sampling of crises that can affect a business

• Equipment failure	• Software virus
• Fire or explosion	• Computer hacking
• Utility breakage	• Civil disturbance
• Transportation accidents	• Terrorism or robbery
• Extended power outage	• Workplace violence
• Earthquake or tsunami	• Vandalism or sabotage
• Geomagnetic storm	• Loss of key company officers
• Tornado, hurricane, winter storm	• Loss of key vendor or customer

One example of this is the 2013 Boston Marathon bombing. The terrorists, brothers Tamerlan Tsarnaev and Dzhokhar Tsarnaev were raised in Kazakhstan and Dagestan when they were Asian republics of the USSR, and in Russia. But they harbored ISIS sympathies like other disaffected Asian militants, and they were self-radicalized after migrating to the U.S. This demonstrates the far-reach that an aberrant ideology can have.

Domestic terrorism in one country can affect neighbors. Regional groups, like the Boko Haram ("People of the Sunnah for Preaching and Jihad Group"), is a Nigerian insurgency that operates primarily in Nigeria but they spill their terror and destruction over to bordering nations.

As in Africa, nations in Europe, the Middle East, the Near East, Asia and the Pacific, have suffered similar attacks by domestic extremists fighting local causes, and the trans-national "Jihad" terror groups acting directly or through regional proxies.

Businesses with offices abroad, business travelers and tourists can be intended targets or hapless victims who get caught in violence. If your company's people travel to or operate abroad frequently, your business continuity plan should consider that when you perform threat and vulnerability assessments.

Directly relevant to our purpose of business continuity and crises management is the fact that organized terrorists and lone wolves increasingly target business centers, shopping centers, hotels, tourism and night spots, sports stadiums, schools, and other places where ordinary people congregate—specifically to kill the greatest number of innocent civilians, sow fear, and portray the government as impotent or malevolent.

The most likely events that can potentially hobble a business, though, are not so dramatic as the previous examples. Businesses are more likely to be hit by mundane yet damaging events like lawsuits, or fire, or industrial accidents.

Figure 1.1 provides a sampling of crises that small- or medium-sized businesses are likely to experience. You should prepare for the ones that could affect you even if the chance is remote.

WHO THIS BOOK IS FOR

Crises are inevitable, whether man-made or natural, or localized to your particular business or one that broadly affects many. They happen all the time. Every business needs to be prepared to avoid, mitigate, or manage the crises that come their way.

Even if one does not visit you early on, take heart in knowing that the time spent preparing for the worst is not wasted; your business continuity preparations are also opportunities to fine-tune your truly essential business processes, and identify company fat you can shed.

Although the principles in this book are applicable to large businesses, it is specifically written for small- to medium-sized enterprises that want to implement a *business continuity management* (BCM) program. It is also suitable for the stand-alone satellite operations of large companies that do not need to be tightly integrated into their corporate parents' plans.

Some manuals employ esoteric formulas and metrics to precisely compare the costs and risks of their potential responses to threats. Here we provide simplified methods to help you quantify your risks in a reasonable way without brain-teasing routines some professional crisis managers might employ. This book is realistic and will meet the practical needs of the average business.

While business continuity management refers to the entire program, to include planning, training and maintenance, the term *business continuity plan* (BCP) refers to the written document that maps your anticipated threats and responses.

Small- and medium-sized organizations also face issues that may not be as critical to larger organizations with respect to planning and preparing for crises, like—

- Financial constraints
- Technological challenges
- Employee resource issues
- Limited knowledge of how to plan

Large companies can also benefit from this simplified system by decentralizing their plans so that the various business units or satellite offices each create a plan to handle their location.

Some federal government agencies with tens of thousands of employees do this by having their district offices and outposts (like embassies) produce their own crisis management plans that are particular to the needs of each satellite operation. Both agencies the author worked for, the F.B.I. and the U.S. State Department, follow this practice.

What the head office can do is to unify the collection of plans from dispersed offices by providing a standard company BCP template and, if necessary, produce one overarching assessment with the many BCPs attached as annexes.

In this we treat the nouns "company," "organization" and "entity" as synonyms. In doing so the author means to include any organization, be it a government agency, a non-profit corporation, a for-profit company or a single-owner business.

PROCEDURAL STEPS TO BUSINESS CONTINUITY

Our approach to business continuity management presents material from the perspective of (a) how crises develop and are normally handled; and (b) the deliverables a crisis manager should prepare to produce a simplified business continuity plan.

Figure 1.2 depicts the danger faced by an organization when a crisis happens and normal operations are disrupted. Communications, data, facilities and critical operations need to be operational for a business to be viable and continue. These are discussed in more detail below.

A crisis does not normally impair all four at once. A storm or major fire could very well disable all four, but most crises deny the company only one or two functions. A computer system crash may only disrupt data processing; an industrial accident can close a facility for some time; or a product tampering incident may affect only critical operations until the crisis is brought under control.

Most crises are less than catastrophic but if they disable or hinder significantly your ability to function normally it is still a crisis.

Communications come first. Without it everything else halts anyway, either because of a physical disconnect or because normal coordination between people and entities remain in chaos without coordination. Communications are the link between geographi-

Figure 1.2: Deploying the business continuity parachute

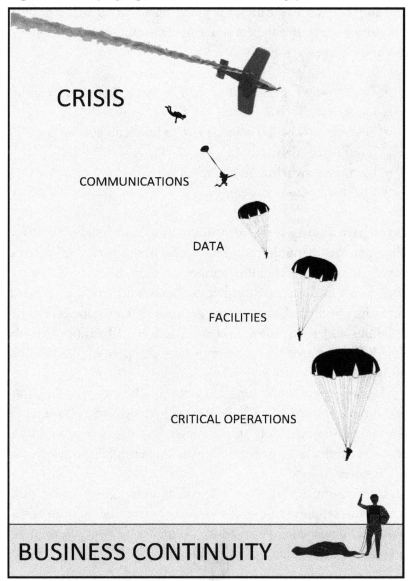

cally separated people and between the computers that share data with remote services or databases.

If communications are damaged, provisional communications

systems will be the first step toward regaining control. Communications breakdowns can occur intentionally, accidentally or by a force of nature, and can be temporary inconveniences or business-threatening events, to wit:

- Entire power grid outages can cause widespread, lengthy blackouts
- Severed or downed voice and data lines can affect a specific building or many city blocks
- Company switchboards can fail
- Specific instruments can fail

Data processing is the next function to restore after communications are reestablished. The modern enterprise, no matter what its size, lives on information—it is its blood; it feeds all aspects of a company's activities. Sales and marketing need client lists and marketing plans. Finance depends on records of liabilities and receivables, and bank ledgers. Operations needs schedules, resource lists, materials lists and pending or fulfilled purchase or work orders. And so on.

A company cannot function without data so it is imperative that the most critical information—that which will keep the company running if only at half speed—be available from duplicate electronic databases *and* in paper form until normal systems are restored.

Information technology (IT) consultants and in-house staff constantly rescue corporate and government clients from technological emergencies caused by accidents, neglect, equipment breakdowns or criminal acts, that lead to—

- loss of power affecting the operation of automated data,
- corruption of databases or other information systems,
- malfunctions of company computer systems like local area networks or servers,

- loss of internet service or email systems, and
- damage to databases by a virus or hacker.

Facilities come next in the hierarchy of needs during a crisis. If the company's normal place of business is unusable then *temporary space* must be available until the affected site is reopened or until a replacement facility is established.

Many events can restrict or prohibit the use of a facility, including natural disasters, wanton criminal acts, civil unrest, or an accident. In many instances your organization may need to reconstitute itself at an alternate site.

Critical operations follow. Once key personnel are talking to each other and they have reasonably current operating data and places to work from, they can begin to carry out the company's most critical functions to maintain the best cash flow possible and stay in touch with clients and suppliers. All other preparations are to make this conduct of critical operations possible.

A side benefit of a business continuity program is that it can also serve to tune up an organization to function more efficiently. By merely identifying and prioritizing its critical operations, a company can take stock of what is truly revenue generating and what is simply supportive or even unnecessary. Companies often find during these exercises that they can save money and accelerate processes by cutting out money-wasting, dispensable tasks.

Before you begin creating your program, you should ask

The modern enterprise, no matter what its size, lives on information—it is its blood; it feeds all aspects of a company's activities.

"A side benefit of a business continuity
program is that it can also serve to tune
up an organization to function more efficiently. By merely identifying and prioritizing its critical operations, a company
can take stock of what is truly revenue
generating and what is simply supportive
or even unnecessary."

---

yourself, "What do we do if we cannot use our facility?" Or ask, "What can I do now to better prepare my business to respond when our facility or information system is unavailable?" Imagine that you have lost the use of your offices and resources normally available to you for day-to-day operations, and plan accordingly.

Less dramatic events that have little to do with tangible equipment or property can threaten a company's survival. An expensive lawsuit, for instance, can wipe a company's earnings and drive it to bankruptcy. Such events, intangible before they occur, will affect the bottom line negatively.

COMPONENTS OF A BUSINESS CONTINUITY PLAN

Once you have considered these questions you are ready to start developing your business continuity program.

Remember that a crisis does not usually cause a business to lose its communications, its data and its facility all at once. It may be the case in the aftermath of a large-scale natural disaster, terrorist act or major fire; but, just as likely a crisis may consist of the loss of just one of these three resources or the loss of a key officer. It is still a crisis but easier to contain.

Finally, while considering ways to mitigate your risks, this book guides you through the preparation of components that are fused into one plan at the conclusion.

Begin with a project plan that details each of the steps you will need to perform. You can replicate Figure 4.1 on page 61 or download ready-made resource templates of all the components, including a project plan template.

Risk Management Program

The risk management program is the one part of the business continuity plan that will likely be used because it is an ongoing audit process aimed to avert or mitigate potential crises.

The vigor and success of your risk management program makes the need to implement the crisis response plan or business continuity strategies less likely. The risk management module normally includes the following components:

- Risk assessment (Figure 5.1 on page 79)
- Risk mitigation strategies (Figure 5.4 on page 84)
- Early warning system (Figure 5.6 on page 90)

Your work creating these components is simplified with the forms provided as Appendices A.3, A.4 and A.5.

Crisis Response Program

This comes into play once a threatening event erupts. It comprises all the actions to be taken during the initial minutes, hours or days after the advent of the emergency.

Other than tasks to trigger government involvement through calls for help, a company's emergency response plan normally should not include the detailed actions expected from government agencies who are charged with public safety.

BUSINESS CONTINUITY IN PUNTA CANA

What if the magnitude of a potential crisis is one that simultaneously affects a number of companies or an entire region, as natural disasters usually do?

The Dominican Republic shares the large island of Hispaniola with Haiti but it occupies most of the territory. Except for services in its capital, Santo Domingo, its government has a weak emergency system and almost no presence in much of the island.

About a fourth of the country's best beaches and natural habitat are remote and far from government services. It's also where the majority of its multitude of luxury resorts lie, and a part of it is in a coastal flood zone in Punta Cana.

The businesses here are on their own and exposed to many threats.

Each of the more than 50 luxury resorts had conceived its own crisis response plan irrespective of the others, and the disjointed results were counterproductive for everyone.

Their common denominator was and is the sole regional energy provider, EGE/Haina, on whom they all rely.

EGE/Haina realized that the area lacked a coordinated omnibus emergency management plan and that the energy provider would be unable to handle the region's energy demand in any kind of crisis.

So EGE/Haina took the initiative to contract with us to conduct research and surveys, produce guides, and hold conferences and workshops to educate the many managers of the multiple resorts and organize them into an emergency cooperative with a common set of crisis management procedures and strategies.

Their mutual concern for the economic health of their region and their industry motivated them to cooperate so that as a community they can perform most of the tasks normally expected from government agencies, like debris removal, flood control, storm shelters and medical services.

But it took one overarching player—in this case the regional energy producer—to champion the cause and guide the many stakeholders to share the cost and cooperate for the common good.

Actions that are the providence of government should be assumed will occur, providing that you considered their capabilities while planning. The BCP can list the expected emergency services along with expected reaction times as planning factors.

This assumes that the company (or satellite office) preparing a plan is located in a region where the government is effective and can dispatch capable crews. Organizations located in regions where government functions are weak or absent will need to plan accordingly. Our sidebar about Punta Cana in the Dominican Republic provides an example.

In normal situations a company's plan should cover what is not the government's responsibility and what is expected of the company to do for themselves within their property and control. The company's initial responsibilities at the outset of a crisis are covered in the following components for managing crises:

- Business continuity strategies (Figure 6.1, page 99)
- Cost-benefit analysis (Figure 6.2, page 103)
- Emergency contacts (Figure 6.3, page 105)
- Crisis response actions (Figure 7.1, page 110)
- Crisis grab kit (Figure 7.2, page 113)

Forms for this component are available as Appendices A.6, A.7, A.8 and A.9 and as downloads. (See page 153.) What is not provided is a form for creating a cost-benefit analysis because this task can vary so much. But Figure 6.2 on page 103 can guide you in creating one.

■   ■   ■

This chapter gives you a preview of the work ahead but before you dive in you should understand what business continuity is about.

The next chapter provides a primer in this subject and summarizes what we call the Risk Intelligence and Solutions Cycle (RISC)™ that, if implemented and practiced, will keep it operating even through crises.

The RISC model and business continuity differ only in scope. As an IT department's "disaster recovery" plan is narrower in scope than the broader concerns of business continuity, so is business continuity narrower in scope than RISC management.

In RISC management incidents need not be potentially crippling or fatal to an organization; if they are abnormal, disruptive or potentially dangerous to some of its people, facilities or processes they probably merit RISC management treatment.

For purposes of this book, though, we recognize that "BCP" is the generally accepted term for "the plan" you need to make your entity resilient.

C H A P T E R

2

BUSINESS CONTINUITY PRIMER

*The illiterate of the 21st Century will not
be those who cannot read and write,
but those who cannot learn,
unlearn, and relearn.*

—Alvin Toffler,
"Future Shock"

WHAT IS A crisis? Ask five business colleagues this question and you will probably get five different answers. But most will agree on a basic commonality: a crisis is any event that can destroy or incapacitate an organization.

This definition could be taken one step further: an event is still a crisis if it interferes with its daily operations so much that it threatens the organization's survival or operating capacity.

If we are to manage a crisis we need to understand how they surface. Even when they seem to appear abruptly they are in fact preceded by a string of warning signs that, if heeded, can reduce or thwart the impact of a looming crisis. They need not be unavoidable "facts of life."

TYPES OF CRISES

Before examining how a crisis can unfold, and the crisis management cycle that can be applied to overcome one, we should first examine the different types of crises.

RECKONING WITH THE FORCES OF NATURE

Mother Nature can be mean and indiscriminate. She will heave our ground and wreck our buildings, swamp our coastal towns and cities, burn our forests. The Sahara, a lush green region only yesterday (in the cosmic time scale), is a vast desert today. Our planet is alive and changing. If we get in the way we pay the price.

Like so many cities, Port-au-Prince, Haiti is built on a fault line. In 2010 a catastrophic magnitude 7.0 earthquake tore the city and surrounding region apart without warning, killed as many as 160,000 and reduced it to rubble.

Other parts of the world have suffered similar destruction. For instance, the great Indian Ocean tsunami of 2004, triggered by sea-floor earthquakes in the Pacific Rim, in one day killed more than 150,000 people in eleven countries.

Massive cyclonic storms like Hurricanes Andrew and Maria can form quickly and wreak destruction in just a few hours.

Wildfires are a normal occurrence and a threat to some of the most attractively forested communities in North America. Massive fires create fast moving fire storms that ravage the towns in their paths.

Millions of acres have burned in British Colombia and California just in recent years. The natural disasters that need to be taken into account to protect your business depends on where you live and work, but this cannot be ignored.

Every year mother nature seems to set new records. Climate warming only ensures that we can expect more, worse disasters.

Nearly all scientists who study the climate observe that human activity is causing very rapid temperature changes, consequently increasing the severity of wind storms, draughts, and floods (that can affect riverside communities); and the polar ice melt will likely inundate coastal cities by 2050.

Natural disasters can appear in the form of hurricanes, tornados, floods, blizzards, electrical storms, geomagnetic storms, sinkholes, mud slides, tsunamis or earthquakes, among others. Any one of these events has the potential to deny an organization of personnel, physical facilities and data. Inaccessibility can last for days, months, or even years.

Even if your business cannot get out of the way of a natural calamity, you can certainly devise early warning systems to trigger mitigation strategies before the disaster happens. The few minutes of warning you get may be enough to avert the worst outcome if you considered the threat and identified a solution when you had time and a clear mind during your planning.

Industrial disasters can be major contaminations, oil spills, explosions, or fires. Small businesses need not consider catastrophes of proportions of the Exxon oil spill near Valdez, Alaska. But many small businesses—gasoline stations, bake shops,

---

A BAKERY GAS LEAK BLOWS UP A SHOPPING MALL

A small pastry shop in the upper floor of a busy shopping mall in Santo Domingo in the Dominican Republic exploded early one morning in 2008. A baker opening for the day started up the oven and ignited a room full of odorless gas that had leaked from a gas line during the night.

Only the baker died because he was the only one in the mall at that very early hour (and security was patrolling outside).

The death toll would have been far more than one if the baker had turned on the ovens just an hour or two later when more employees of the pastry shop and nearby stores would have been at their work stations.

The explosion blew up a section of the small, multi-level mall's roof and demolished the pastry shop and scores of neighboring stores.

With the loss of life and lacking adequate insurance against such massive loss, the pastry shop and some other businesses in the mall did not recover.

The quarter of the mall where the pastry shop had been took months to rebuild.

welding shops, dry cleaners, lumberyards and printers, to name a few—deal with substances and supplies that can contaminate or be radioactive, combustible or explosive. An industrial accident could affect them or their neighbors severely.

Health-based crises are similar to industrial disasters, but for the job-related aspects of the event. Job-related health issues can affect a small business especially if they are in health care or emergency services, or they may be in some other line of business, such as security screening, where their personnel are in constant contact with potentially infected people. Conversely, a business must be on guard to prevent its workers from passing on diseases to customers, visitors or other employees.

CHIPOTLE MEXICAN GRILL FOOD POISONING

In 2015, the chain restaurant Chipotle Mexican Grill had to close 43 of their restaurants in the states of Washington and Oregon because of an E. coli outbreak that infected 55 customers and hospitalized at least 21.

Most of the company's restaurants reopened after deep cleaning and implementing new food handling procedures, but the business has suffered.

Chipotle's stock traded as high as almost $800 per share at the time of this outbreak, and tumbled 20% in the days after the company closed its infected restaurants.

After this initial devaluation Chipotle's stock continued a downward trend for two years to under $400 per share.

How much the E. coli outbreak contributed to the continuing losses isn't clear but it wasn't until after 2018 that its stock regained most of its pre-incident value.

A business can also find itself in a health crisis if a contaminant like asbestos were discovered in the building they occupy, perhaps after one of their employees is diagnosed with cancer. Questions will probably surface then as to whether or not the company knew or should have known about the hazard.

Another health threat to a business is an epidemic, a fast-breaking contagious disease in your region, or a pandemic if it spreads to other countries. An epidemic or pandemic will affect not just your organization but thousands or millions of other businesses at the same time and will cause widespread disruption to everyday life.

In just the last one hundred years the world's population has quadrupled exponentially from 1.8 billion to nearly eight billion. Modern transportation now moves a constant stream of travelers halfway around the world in less than a day. Any contagious outbreak anywhere in the world can become an epidemic or a pandemic in just weeks if not quickly contained.

A brief history of recent pandemics (Pinon, 2010) gives us an idea of just how increasingly vulnerable we really are: in 1918, even before the advent of airlines, the H1N1 virus, the so-called "Spanish Flu," infected about 500 million people and killed 40 to 50 million (just in the U.S. it took 675,000 lives); the "Asian Flu" of 1957 that killed two million people began in East Asia and quickly spread to Hong Kong and the United States (where 100,000 died); the H3N2 virus known as "Hong Kong Flu" originated in China in 1968 and killed one million people; in 2002, 8,000 cases of SARS-CoV (Severe Acute Respiratory Syndrome) thought to originate from bats, spread to 22 countries and killed 800 people; and in 2009 the "Swine Flu" pandemic, a "novel" version of the H1N1 virus, surged in the U.S. and Mexico and quickly spread around the world to infect over 60 million people and kill 575,000 worldwide (and over 12,000 in the U.S.).

This looks only at influenza like epidemics. There are many other highly communicable diseases now under control, like ebola, measles, cholera, and AIDS, not to mention mutations of these or "novel" ones we have yet to experience and name.

If we look at the general trend of this we see that fatality rates for new epidemics seem to have decreased with time thanks to modern medicine, awareness and better crisis management.

We should also sense a time pattern and expect that pandemics are occurring more frequently, perhaps at ten to fifteen year intervals now, probably due to the world's growing populations and increased travel and interactions.

An outbreak need not occur in your area directly to stress your business into a crisis if your supply line extends to contaminated areas. At best, such health crises may restrict your employees' business travels and your production may slow because of a disrupted supply chain. At worst, your organization may suffer personnel losses (to sickness or layoffs) and you may be forced to operate primarily from remote locations through a skeleton workforce and with a reduced demand for your product.

Unless you have the foresight to assure that a supply of resources will be on hand when needed, like medical supplies and services for healthcare and raw materials for production, you are unlikely to get them once the crisis starts. Like natural disasters, such events will force you to compete with other organizations for scarce resources at the worst possible time.

Equipment/production breaks are increasingly common with the advent of complex, electronic systems. Information and service companies rely almost entirely on data and the digital data systems that store them. But other problems can beset a small or large company: major product defects, major distribution breakdowns, security lapses, or product defects. Each of these can cause a crisis.

A small business need not rely on electronic networks to be vulnerable. If your business in manufacturing, food services or transportation, it probably owns vehicles or machinery that can malfunction and bring the business to a halt, or cause injuries; or a bakery's leaking gas system could ignite. Prevention and mitigation depends on awareness, safety procedures, maintenance and inspections.

Image and reputation injuries to any size company can occur when incidents such as the Enron-Anderson Consulting fraud scandal involve a business; or if the mishaps occur repeatedly giving the impression that the issue is a company-wide problem, as when Chipotle Mexican Grill food poisoning outbreaks repeated themselves in different restaurants. The entire brand's reputation and finances can suffer if the incidents are not quickly controlled.

Human resources issues may not immediately strike as a wellspring of crises events but they have the potential for it. Some HR issues that can hurt a business are employee misconduct whether or not it affects other employees, or a company's own policies (or lack of them) that can lead to conflicts with its personnel. A company's ineffective HR can lead to damaging publicity and expensive lawsuits by its personnel.

ANDERSON CONSULTING-ENRON BANKRUPTCY

Anderson Consulting's size may have been what kept the consulting giant from collapsing totally in the wake of financial irregularities that culminated in the 2001 bankruptcy of its client, the Enron Corporation, and the convictions of several top officers from both companies, including Arthur Anderson, who colluded with Enron to cook their books and destroy documentary evidence of fraud.

Anderson Consulting survived as a company only after the expulsions of Arthur Anderson, its founder, and several other Anderson top officers; a name change to Accenture (with a new logo); and big reductions in size and marketplace importance.

It took drastic measures and many years of rebuilding a new brand for Accenture to reclaim its former prestige.

Small or middle-sized businesses would not fare as well.

A company's survival is also threatened when officers or key personnel are suddenly absent due, perhaps, to an accident, natural death, or a wave of resignations. A personnel crisis can spawn a parallel image/reputation crisis.

Terrorism, once a threat that primarily targeted governments and society's prominent, now can indiscriminately affect any business, large, small or micro. A business might be targeted because of its symbolism, or it can just be in the wrong place.

Terrorism today no longer is the purview of organized, well-funded groups of hundreds or thousands of "fighters" like al-Qaeda and ISIL, or domestic terrorists like the Aryan Nations or the Ku Klux Klan. The abbreviated chronology of terrorist events in page 7 gives us a good idea of how this threat can affect people and organizations, small or large, with increasing frequency and damage.

Lone wolves, radicalized individuals who sympathize and act on their own in the name of a cause they embrace, or who develop

SEPTEMBER 11 ATTACKS: A NEW NORMAL

The infamous September 11th (9/11) terrorist attack on the World Trade Center caught nearly everyone off guard. It caused a paradigm shift in public safety everywhere, not only in the U.S. where the attacks took place. The entire world has been thrown into a new normal, especially for the traveling public.

Warning signals of the looming attack were evident for several years before it happened. An increasing volley of mass violence against U.S. embassies and a U.S. Navy ship, captured al-Qaeda members, propaganda releases meant to stir violent zealots, intercepted terrorism plans around the world—and an earlier, 1993 bombing of the World Trade Center itself, although that first attempt failed to cause great damage to the Towers—all were harbingers of what was to come in 2001: the massive destruction of entire city blocks at the World Trade Center in New York.

The business victims ranged from street corner vendors to Wall Street monoliths.

Our then-decentralized intelligence system was incapable of grouping all the evidence onto one scale so their total weight could be felt. Instead, the tell-tale signs were dispersed and isolated throughout various agencies. Had one agency had more of the puzzle pieces to look at simultaneously the attack might well have been discovered and prevented.

Although the new system is still imperfect, a repeat of such an event is far less likely today because of it.

their own radical philosophy, also can be threats to businesses.

A nation's early warning system (the intelligence community) generally cannot detect and identify lone wolves until they have committed an attack because lone wolves' planning and preparations are self-contained. They do not communicate and conspire with others so the counter-terrorism agencies normally cannot pick up "signals" of a developing event. The usual means of detection—surveillances of conspirators, informants, technical intercepts, captured documents, etc.—are generally ineffective against lone wolves.

When lone wolves are discovered ahead of an act it is usually

---

PULSE NIGHTCLUB SLAUGHTER IN FLORIDA

A self-radicalized U.S.-born man of Arabic descent walked into the Pulse nightclub, a gay locale in Orlando, Florida in 2016 carrying an assault rifle and a semi-automatic pistol.

He immediately started shooting and killing, then trapped most of the patrons inside as hostages.

During his attack he called 9-1-1 and then a local television station and declared his allegiance to ISIS and his sympathy for the Boston Marathon bombings.

The police investigation did not establish homophobia as a motive. They did learn that the shooter had cased several businesses in the area and apparently chose to target Pulse, possibly because it was packed with people.

After the initial minutes of shooting randomly at patrons he stopped and barricaded himself in the club with the remaining people as hostages. After about three hours he was killed by a SWAT team.

Before it was over, the shooter had killed 49 club patrons and injured 53 more.

When a quick-thinking club bouncer first heard the shooting he immediately moved to open a back door to let more than 70 patrons escape.

We have no reason to think that the bouncer's valiant actions were premeditated in a club BCP, but there's a lesson here for businesses composing a plan: be sure to identify and establish as many escape routes as possible in case a fast evacuation is needed out of closed quarters, and be sure that staff knows and practices the plan.

an unrelated arrest, or a traffic stop, or a search warrant that discovers evidence of bomb-making, weapons or suspicious documents, or an accidental explosion.

Criminal attacks can have a greater impact on a small business than a large one, but no one is immune. Common robberies and workplace shootings, sabotage to company facilities, product tampering, counterfeiting and piracy, all belong to this category. These events can become damaging crises by driving away fearful customers, or if media channels are not handled correctly.

ANTHRAX ATTACKS AGAINST AMERICAN MEDIA, INC.

Gun violence is not the only way a business can be attacked. Biological agents are another way to harm a business. These are less common but are, potentially, more damaging.

For instance, the 2001 anthrax mailings to American Media, Inc. (publishers of the National Inquirer tabloid) in Boca Raton, Florida, and to the U.S. Senate and to a U.S. post office in Washington, D.C., resulted in five deaths, among them an editor for American Media.

An important BCP point here, though, is that American Media's corporate offices went from normal operations in one minute to an evacuated, empty, quarantined building the next when the anthrax powder was discovered in the mail room. Soon after the evacuation, officials *condemned* the building. This criminal attack suddenly left the company without its equipment, physical records, or work spaces and with lives lost.

In time the company reestablished itself in completely new physical facilities elsewhere (in New York, New York) because they could never reoccupy their contaminated former building.

Cyber attacks are also criminal but their virtual, nebulous nature differentiates them from traditional crime. The objectives of cyber attacks can be simple malice against indiscriminate victims; revenge against a specific target, such as an employer or a company believed to have wronged the attacker; or the outright theft of money or information that can be monetized.

A growing cyber crime that affects businesses of all sizes, from mom-and-pops to large institutions, is *ransomware* attacks. A recent study by Osterman Research (2017) determined that one out of five small businesses attacked with ransomware were driven to failure. Cyber criminals operating from countries like Nigeria or Russia, or elsewhere in the world, gain access through the Internet to a business' server and infect it with code that encrypts the files and denies the victim business access to its own database.

A demand for payment in cyber currency follows—in exchange for the decryption "key" to regain access. After being paid a ransom the extortionist may or may not provide the victim with the promised key. Unless a ransomware victim has a clean backup of the files the victim usually has no choice but to comply with the extortion demand.

RANSOMWARE DRIVES WOOD RANCH MEDICAL TO FAILURE

A prominent California healthcare provider in 2019 joined a growing list of small businesses that closed their doors due to ransomware attacks.

5,835 (nearly all) of the clinic's patient records in their servers were encrypted and its computer systems were permanently damaged in the attack. The malware code even reached and encrypted the clinic's backup files, leaving the clinic with no way to recover their files.

The healthcare center acceded and paid the demanded ransom but the extortionist failed to give the clinic the decryption key. The clinic was unable to recover and was forced to cease operations.

Their investigation of the attack concluded that the attacker's objective was to extract the hefty ransom and not, apparently, to steal sensitive patient information. Because of the uncertainty the clinic has to assume the worst and act as though patients' records were compromised. So they are assisting the thousands of affected patients with identity theft prevention and credit history monitoring.

Lesson: businesses must establish backup practices and channels that are independent and divorced of the central database so that an attack on does not leak over to backups. Unaffected backups would have saved the files.

The most dangerous and consequential cyber attacks, though, are insidious cyber penetrations by well-funded and resourceful foreign state actors who spy on or sabotage political, economic or military targets. And their inroads tend to be through businesses of any size that work on government contracts, especially for defense or national security agencies. But any business that holds interesting intellectual property, or operates in a critical industry such as communications or energy, to name only two, can come under cyber attack by a nefarious foreign agency.

Proprietary information losses can be severe. The risk is especially true if the company produces only one service or product. Diversity only lessens the impact of such a loss.

Other types of information that affect the entire company is the loss of customer lists, vendor/supplier lists, production schedules, proposals and project bids, pricing schedules, formulas and processes, among others. Each of these represents company information that is valuable to competitors.

Corporate espionage and intellectual property theft or

INTELLECTUAL PROPERTY THEFT FROM DURA-BAR, INC.

Robert O'Rourke was the longtime metallurgist and a manager at Dura-Bar, a Chicago area manufacturer of cast-iron products.

O'Rourke was arrested in 2018 by the F.B.I. for stealing his company's metallurgy trade secrets for the benefit of a Chinese competitor. The competitor had offered O'Rouke a top position in China with their company for the trade secrets O'Rourke had access to.

Just days before he quit his Dura-Bar job he downloaded and copied a slew of Dura-Bar documents.

He was arrested at the airport just as he prepared to board with the company's most valuable trade secrets. The loss of these secrets would have hurt Dura-Bar financially as they would have lost valuable technology and customers to the Chinese competitor.

Lesson: businesses need to be aware of employee conduct and sensitize its staff to recognize and report suspicious behavior.

mishandling can result in huge actual or potential revenue losses that can become a crisis. Keep in mind that foreign businesses that have no assets to expose in the country your business is in (where you may have legal recourse) are unlikely to observe your laws. And they may not even if they do have assets there.

Sensitive information losses of legally protected data can result in severe financial distress to a business and its clients.

Sensitive information is about your customers' (or employees') personal data, like numbers for bank accounts, credit cards, social security or health care benefits; your company's internal number for a customer (if that can be used to order products or services in the customer's name); passwords; or records about their health, education or finances. These are not all inclusive and they are sensitive by themselves.

Sensitive information thieves use a long supply chain, from procurement, the actual theft from a wallet or a data repository, to deployment, the actual use of stolen information to buy things or draw money in the victim's identity.

Stolen personal information may go through many hands

THEFT OF 13,000 RECORDS FROM A FLORIDA CLINIC

Three men, one of them the administrative employee of a Tampa, Florida pediatric medical practice (the insider), were arrested in 2017 and convicted in 2018 on charges of conspiracy and aggravated identity theft and fraud.

The employee had access to the clinic's more than 13,000 patient medical records housed in a centralized database that included personally identifiable informa-tion (PII); that is, sensitive information about the patients, their parents and their guardians.

The ring was found in possession of the PII of over 13,000 individuals' records that the insider stole and that the conspirators used to fraudulently apply for and use credit cards, and to file false tax returns in the name of the victims. The three shared in the proceeds.

before its illicit nature is discovered. And, somewhere between procurement and deployment, the thieves will likely use the obscure "dark web" to cover their tracks or to sell their data loot to other criminals.

A pure hack (using no insider's help) into an electronic database is not so likely. Instead, hackers will start their break into your system by using information they know about the intended victim to fool a company employee into thinking the hacker (calling in) is the customer requesting help, and thus be granted password changes, services, or additional sensitive information. This is known as "social engineering."

An easier path to information theft is to work with an accomplice inside your company who will sell to the outsider copies of records in your paper or electronic files, like an automobile dealer's customers' applications for loans, or credit card account numbers your company may keep for recurring charges.

We give this risk a good deal of attention here because identity theft is an exploding, chronic crime problem everywhere in the world. Unbeknownst to most companies, they hold sensitive information and fail to recognize it as such, and most don't know how to properly protect it or that they are required to.

If your company holds sensitive information you can mitigate the risk by controlling access to the data repositories; conducting reliable, periodic background screenings before and after the hire; requiring fraud awareness training at least for the personnel with access to the repositories, if not everyone; and establishing a robust audit trail.

For businesses in highly regulated industries, like health care, education or financial services, it's very likely that one or more federal[1] or state laws require that your company have an

---

1 The principal federal laws that apply to sensitive information security are the Fair Credit Reporting Act (FCRA) and its related Fair and Accurate Credit Transactions Act (FACTA) and Red Flags Rule for protecting consumer information; the Gramm-Leach-Bliley Act (GLBA) for protecting financial information; the Health Insurance Portability and Accountability Act (HIPAA) for protecting medical information; and the Family Educational Records Protection Act (FERPA) for protecting educational records.

information security program.

The good news is that doing your due diligence—establishing and maintaining a legally-compliant *information security program*—will help protect your business from charges of negligence when your customers' identity theft cases trace back to your business as the point of origin.

Economic threats can take the form of boycotts, strikes, hostile takeovers, or stock devaluations. Each can cripple an organization financially, or can hurt its reputation or image. For instance, an outsider seeking to gain from a contrived price drop can manipulate a company's stock value. A company's value can also suffer because of officer misconduct.

Companies employing personnel from labor unions have to consider the differences in their own agenda and that of the unions'. Distrust and ideological (cultural) differences abound between labor and management. Strikes and plant shutdowns are a constant threat to the efficient production regimens that businesses need to survive.

MARTHA STEWART LIVING OMNIMEDIA STOCK DEVALUATION

In 2001 InClome, a drug company developing an experimental antibody, was denied an expected approval from the Food and Drug Administration.

A criminal investigation ensued when it was revealed that many of the company's executives had sold their stocks just before the FDA announcement, giving rise to suspicions of insider trading.

The investigation led to a stock broker who handled the trades of the InClome executives. The broker then confessed that he had tipped off Martha Stewart, one of his principal clients, of the impending InClome price drop, and helped her sell off her holdings before the FDA announcement.

Martha Stewart, a very successful television personality and the founder of Martha Stewart Living OmniMedia, went to jail for several years for her part and her company sold for $353 million, a fraction of the company's former valuation of $2 billion.

Legal challenges such as a major corporate lawsuit, an individual or class-action lawsuits by present or former employees, a defec-
tive product, a service error or omission, lawsuits from vendors or
distributors, or malfeasance by company officers, can happen to any
business. The Anderson Consulting and the Martha Stewart cases
are examples of legal challenges that can drive a business into bankruptcy or devaluation.

Regulatory environment crises tend to affect new applications of existing products or the introduction of new ones. They
may conflict with social customs expressed are laws or ordi-
nances. And they may displace or challenge established competitors who may seek government intervention to protect their turf.

   Government regulates more and more industries every year.
Those in health care, finance, law, to name a few, must interpret
and apply myriad laws and regulations meant to control business
behavior in the best interest of all.

   It's difficult enough to operate a business in a mature industry. Usually there is case law from previous government challenges that define the permissible from the impermissible. But

---

ELECTRIC SCOOTERS CAUSE REGULATORY JAMS

Our cities are chocked with auto-
mobiles. So, the search is on for
environmentally friendly alternatives. Enter swarms of electric
scooters with names like Lime,
Lyft, Spin, Bird, Scoot and Skip.

   But those ubiquitous two-
wheelers are rolling uphill in
places because they are a newly
discovered mode of transportation and some have jumped into
markets without city permits.

Other concerns that munic-
ipalities may need to resolve
and codify, where they may
operate, and where they may be
prohibited.

   Some scooter companies have
also failed to follow certain zoning
laws, or have allowed for scooters
to pile up and block sidewalks.
And that causes complaints and
headaches while we adjust to the
new.

rapidly changing industries such as high technology and communications constantly create new opportunities —new business models—not foreseen by existing regulations.

Cutting-edge companies pushing on the envelope are likely to be singled out for action when old regulations do not address a changed environment. They may ask the courts to promulgate new interpretations given new technology. Either way, cutting-edge firms may need to fight regulators and competitors in court.

IT'S WISE TO RISC YOUR BUSINESS

No, we didn't misspell "risk" in the heading of this section. RISC (pronounced "risk") stands for Risk Intelligence and Solutions Cycle," our holistic approach to business continuity and crisis management that's illustrated in Figure 2.1 on page 38. Now we'll discuss why you'll want to adopt a RISC program to assure the survival and continuation of your business through crises you may be presented.

Understand, though, that a crisis is not necessarily the initial event itself; it bears repeating that the greatest damage from a crisis results from the negative consequences of poor preparation and inappropriate reactions to the event.

The first thing in order when a crisis emerges is to activate the organization's crisis management team (CMT)—and set the plan in motion.

If the organization has not prepared for emergencies and has no CMT, then the crisis is exacerbated from the outset. If it is fast breaking, this will only add to the burden and reaction time, or it will go undone and the event will be managed *ad hoc*, compounding the crisis.

If your crisis is localized or particular to your company, the media may be on your heels almost as it happens. How you handle their intrusion may well dictate how your company will be portrayed to the public.

Figure 2.1: Risk intelligence and solutions cycle (RISC)™

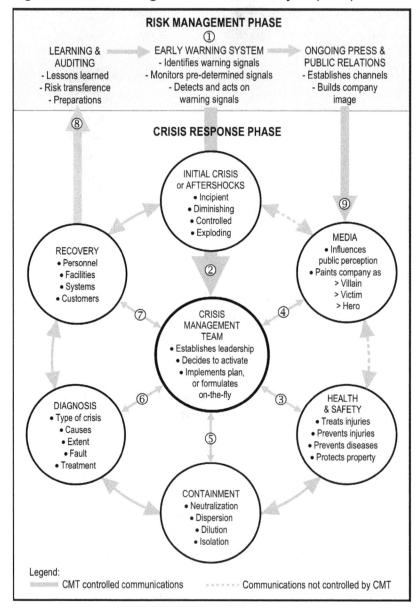

Figure 2.1 enumerates the suggested sequence for actions. First, companies should accept the inevitability of crises and

prepare for them during the risk management phase (①). Companies that have not gone through one will have more work in store producing the first BCP.

The first step is to audit the company to determine its preparedness. That means determining its crisis management (CM) strengths and shoring up the weaknesses. Part II of this book (Process) is designed to help you conduct your first audit and produce your first BCP document in the shortest possible time.

The establishment of an early warning system is most important prior to a crisis. The company needs to articulate what signals are important to it and why. For example, an unexplained rise in "intermittent employee sickness reports" in a household cleaning products factory may indicate a slow, toxic leak in their chemicals storage system. Or, a "10% rise in robberies" in the area, particularly if neighboring businesses have been victimized, may well call for a review of the company's own defenses.

Another important preparatory step is to create a portfolio of thoughtful, generic press releases for each type of crisis that the firm could face. These press drafts can then be customized with minor modifications without time loss when the need arises.

Establishing good relations with the media, through press releases, liaison and cooperation; and directly with the public (e.g., chambers of commerce and charities) is another important step in your overall business continuity program. Communications channels and sympathetic contacts to inform stakeholders and the public will be of great value when things turn ugly (⑨) and they will help paint you as a victim, if not a hero, rather than a villain.

In reality, your organization will face several crises at once, each giving rise to another crisis if mishandled. A violent crime on the company's premises can result in lost customers and revenues, which can lead to financial disruption and lawsuits, and in turn to a tarnished image and, perhaps, insolvency. This fact is one of the best arguments for having an existing business continuity plan that has been rehearsed and tested before a crisis happens, and a standing CMT— ready to spring into action (②) when a crisis arises. Each member of the team has pre-designated functions they can execute in rehearsed concert.

Priority conflicts can and will arise. In such cases, stick to the three basics, in this order, until you get the crisis under control:

③   **treat** injuries, save lives and promote public safety;

④   **inform** the media and the company's leadership; and,

⑤   **contain** the crisis (neutralize, disperse, dilute or isolate).

The dotted arrows in Figure 2.1 depict the media's place and space during *your* crisis. Media outfits will be on scene in public places and, with your permission, in your facilities, as soon as they sense a crisis. They will be anywhere they have access to looking to interview your employees, clients, responders—anyone who can comment about it.

It will behoove you (or your company's designated media representative) to be the media's *first* source of information and to set a cooperative tone. This is also where your pre-crisis media relations efforts will realize their best dividends. Good corporate citizenship you may have exercised, your own good news releases, and their favorable media coverage about your company prior to a crisis, may serve as a foundation for you and for your media contacts to frame the crisis in the most favorable light possible.

A diagnosis (⑥) of the emergency will soon be in line for the following rounds when newer media releases can begin to refine first round statements. But recovery (⑦) can only be effected once it is clear that the crisis is well under control.

Diagnosis and recovery strategies will go through a series of refinements that address a changing environment influenced by the appropriateness of your initial actions, media coverage, and one or more aftershocks usually born from your actions, statements, and media-generated perceptions.

Each aftershock presents a smaller, related crisis that complicates the situation and lengthens the crisis' time frame.

Aftershocks can be prevented or mitigated through sound,

pre-conceived strategies (presented as the business continuity plan) that catapult a pre-designated and rehearsed crisis management team (CMT) at the first sign of an *incipient* crisis. (This is where the match has been struck, or the fuse has been lit.) It is better to misread warning signs and act proactively (blow out the match, or cut the fuse) than to react to a *breaking* (exploding) crisis.

> "A crisis is not necessarily the initial event itself; rather, the greatest damage from a crisis results from the negative consequences of poor preparation and inappropriate reactions to the event."

Treating the injured or endangered does not pertain only to humans; it also applies to wildlife and other animals, and the environment. You can be sure that, regardless of how a crisis starts or where fault lies, the company's behavior and sincerity during the event will be scrutinized. Arrogance, self-righteousness or secrecy in the eyes of the media or public will damn the company regardless of fault.

The point here is that a company undergoing a crisis had better show—first and foremost—great concern for its employees, the public, wildlife and the environment.

A crisis need not be an industrial accident, or an act of extreme violence, to require health and safety considerations. Many corporate crises are of a different nature: They may suffer severe financial setbacks, or even bankruptcy, because of a fraud scandal or the accidental loss of one or more of their key officers.

Companies whose executives are blamed of greed, mismanagement or callousness toward the company, its employees or public are likely to compound problems that would otherwise be surmountable. Your own employees will add fuel to the fire (with inside information, theft, sabotage, slowdowns or strikes) if they perceive themselves as dispensable.

Liability is another issue. Each injury, each death, each trauma, adds to the final bill. So, aside from actually caring for the human condition, it is very much in the company's interest to do everything possible to preserve or regain the health and safety of everyone touched by the crisis.

Once recovery is well under way the organization should immediately also move to the crisis' final step: return to the risk mitigation phase (⑧) to assess the company's crisis management performance and prepare for future events by producing lessons learned documentation, adjusting the BCP and, very importantly, train personnel, retrain and retrain them again with an improved system.

■ ■ ■

Crisis management does not guarantee you can prevent all crises but it does provide well-conceived strategies to mitigate them, and for recovery in a minimum of time.

C H A P T E R

3

CASE STUDIES

Human beings, who are almost unique
in having the ability to learn from the
experience of others, are also remarkable
for their apparent disinclination to do so.

— Douglas Adams

O NE TRIED AND true method for tackling a new challenge is to study how others have done it. This chapter presents case studies for three businesses: two small and one medium-sized. The names of these companies and some circumstances have been changed to protect proprietary information and methods but the issues and strategies presented are mostly factual.

Here we present the principal threats and weaknesses they identified and the solutions they used to become more resilient. You'll probably see the most parallels with one of these companies. You can borrow ideas and apply them to your planning, and use our forms and templates to give you a jump start.

ANDREWS & BATES CONSULTING, LLC

Andrews & Bates Consulting, LLC (ABC) is a small, growing member-managed business with four partners that was established about ten years ago. It currently has only five employees at the head office: a managing partner with decades of operational experience in the company's line of business, a second managing partner experienced in marketing and sales, a full-time projects manager, an accounting technician, and a full-time secretary. Two other employees, who function as analysts and consultants, currently work on a part-time basis only.

By agreement, all four partners take part in decision-making and share in the company's profits. Additionally, the two full-time managing partners are also paid a salary.

The remainder of ABC's workforce consists of a large network of contractors and independent affiliates around the country that telecommute with ABC or travel directly to job sites in their region to execute consulting contracts.

Infrastructure

With its remote workforce, ABC's physical space needs are modest. On the other hand, it relies greatly on its Internet-based intranet for collaboration, dependable communications and electronic databases as its product line is a variety of consulting reports on business processes. It must be able to collect, manipulate, sort, store, retrieve and communicate in a variety of ways: through the Internet, faxes, a cloud-based storage system, and even by telephone or in person.

ABC is situated in a rented suite in the tenth floor, managed by an executive office suites company in a twelve-story building with only basic security services. It is not in a known flood area and the building has withstood several hurricanes, the primary natural threat in the company headquarters' region.

Like most commercial office buildings, ABC's building has a great deal of glass facing the streets, but building management takes measures to protect this exposure when windstorms threaten it. Even so, ABC occupies an inside office suite and has no glass windows that could break in the event of a hurricane. Essentially, ABC's office and equipment are sheltered from nature's forces; so natural disasters are low in its list of concerns.

Apart from potential windstorm damage, the one physical threat to ABC's offices, a common concern for all of the building's tenants, is fire. ABC must consider that it could suffer fire damage, or water damage if the fire control sprinkler system activates. ABC's computers are likely to suffer irreparable damage in such an event but its data is stored with a major cloud-based service that triplicates (backs up) its customers' data holdings in three different parts of the world.

Except for temporary working documents that also reside in notebook computers that synchronize with the cloud, ABC holds no significant paper archives to damage or to lose, and it keeps a local physical backup of its "database in the cloud" on one external drive in the home office of a managing partner.

Perceived Vulnerabilities

ABC LLC is a highly-specialized company where the marketing manager and the projects manager are continually learning some of the tasks performed primarily by its operations manager; that is, the final observations and recommendations that add value and competitive advantage to ABC's projects, are still based on the operations manager's professional experience.

Losing the marketing manager's skills and market relationships would hamper the company but would not cripple it as her absence would not interrupt present operations, and marketing talent is easier to find. But, ABC's continuity as a viable business with the marketing manager alone is questionable if the operations manager were unable to perform his functions.

The next most critical vulnerability would be permanent data loss, particularly data for unfinished projects that would need to be redone. Such a crisis would easily result in late projects and unhappy clients, not to mention the cost to the company of repeating the work lost.

As with many businesses, ABC's third vulnerability is cash flow. This is where the company's marketing and sales activities are important. To assure its continuation, ABC must maintain a continuous stream of work and revenues, and it currently does not have the six-month cash reserves that would be prudent for any business to have. In a financial crisis it would need to revert to a credit line that it currently does not have.

The company has a small customer base and more than half of its revenues are derived from just two major clients. The loss of either account would cause a severe interruption to its cash flow, and if not restored within two months, the company would need to reduce its overhead radically and become a home-based business again, or become insolvent.

A lawsuit due to an error or omission in its work product is another event that would threaten its financial well-being as it would incur out-of-pocket costs, much higher insurance premiums, and would be a serious distraction.

When ABC's risk assessment was completed using the figures and tables in this workbook, four issues emerged as clear and urgent threats to the company's well-being. Following the process described in chapter five in which potential crises that score above 30 should be considered worrisome, the highest score (84) was for the loss of the key officer, followed by incurring a significant cash flow shortfall (75) or a major client (revenue) loss (60) because such events portend lowered credit ratings or insolvency.

Finally, a communications disruption, the loss of its projects manager (a key employee), a lawsuit, and the loss of a key client, all scored high enough to be of concern (36, 32, 36 and 30, respectively).

Risk Management

This company identified a number of strategies to mitigate or resolve its weaknesses. For example:

- it embarked on a number of actions to diversify its client base through marketing and is becoming less reliant on the two major accounts;

- it accelerated the cross-training of its marketing and projects managers to better understand and perform most of the operations manager's contributions;

- it recruited a fifth partner/shareholder whose experience and professional certifications could supplant the operations partner in his absence;

- it is considering a business owner's policy (BOP) to transfer much of the risk pertaining to errors and omissions, accident, protracted revenue losses, and liability, to an insurance company;

- it is building liaison channels with media representatives and its partners have become active in different, local chambers of commerce to better serve the community and foster good will;

- it instituted a program to write a series of policy memos and manuals to guide company ethics and procedures as a guard against a leadership vacuum and lawsuits;

- it signed up for an inexpensive, alternate telephone-based (hot spot) 5G internet carrier to augment its fiber optic-based primary company);

- it replaced its accounting system from a localized desktop computer-based application with a cloud-based Software-as-a-Service (SaaS) accounting system;

- it supplied 5G cellular telephone service to all its officers to establish a redundant communications system that can supplant its normal VoIP telephone service; and,

- it purchased a fire extinguisher for its suite and procured a copy of the building emergency plan from its landlord.

To cap its risk mitigation program, ABC LLC also established an early warning system that, among other things, monitors client feedback through calls and surveys, cloud-based computer systems and backups, and the media.

Crisis Response Preparations

ABC identified and prioritized the list of functions that it must perform in the event of a crisis in order to stay in business and recover. As would be expected, above all it must perform the existing revenue generating work, create invoices and deliver reports to its clients.

On-hand job intake and assignments would be the second priority, followed by notifying clients and vendors of the nature and expected duration of the emergency. The rest are of secondary importance until the crisis is resolved.

ALL COLORS PRINTING COMPANY

The All Colors Printing Company (All Colors) is a successful family-owned private corporation that serves clients primarily within the county where it is located. It has been in business for over forty years and has a payroll of fifteen employees, including several of the family's members.

Each of the positions already have more than one person who can perform the duties of any absent employee, so succession, attrition and absences due to normal life events (like maternity leave, health care or vacations) can be handled as long as most of the crew presents to work. But the simultaneous loss or absence of more than one third of the personnel would curtail job fulfillment.

Infrastructure

All Colors is located about midway in a long, flat-roofed one-story strip office building along a well-trafficked boulevard.

The company is vulnerable to severe tropical weather due to its location on the ground floor in low-lying land. Its store front glass is protected by a decorative see-through brick wall but not by hurricane shutters even though it is in a hurricane danger area. The company's glass windows could be broken during a hurricane if high speed debris flew through the brick facade. In sum, the shop is not adequately protected against severe storms.

All Colors has a standard telephone system and its employees also have personal cellular smartphones. Its largest investment in equipment is in a sophisticated bank of computers that is used for computerized graphics design and publication layouts.

Their work product is stored digitally on hard drives that are regularly backed up and kept in a fire and waterproof safe in the shop. Until recently backups were stored in the principal's residence and not in a different geographic location or in the cloud.

Being a printing company, it must store flammable liquids and paper in its premises and potentially dangerous equipment, like cutters, are also kept on site and are used frequently. So workplace safety has been on their agenda for some time. They have mitigated these potential hazards through proper storage practices and insurance.

Perceived Vulnerabilities

All Colors is a traditional, established print shop with steady clientele; so, it does not feel vulnerable to a revenue interruption. Having followed the research steps outlined in chapter five, it identified only four threats to their business. Still, the company has been mitigating those risks and finds that the final risk level, after taking into account its available internal and external resources to mitigate them, lowers their exposure to acceptable levels. Nevertheless, All Colors chose to mitigate these moderate dangers even more.

The print shop's greatest risk is from hurricane damage, with a score of 80, which is nearly a "high risk" on our scale ("Table 5.4: Suggested scoring chart" on page 83). Given the see-through brick wall and waterproofing precautions they would take in the face of a storm, All Colors has not felt compelled to purchase hurricane shutters.

Risk Management

Before the workshop All Colors did not feel particularly vulnerable to disruptive events. They did not have a clear idea of why; only that they felt comfortable. But when asked how they would react to different types of risks or crisis, their responses were typical uncertainty and simplicity.

Even though they confirmed that their risk of business disruption and failure was low they were glad to have gone through a RISC/BCP workshop. It motivated All Colors to successfully mitigate nearly all of its risks on its own. Their participation in the exercises articulated and quantified their level of preparedness.

All Colors' risk mitigation strategies stayed nearly unchanged. They had transferred risk through proper insurance policies, leadership succession was well planned for, their small staff was cross-trained, their flammable supplies were safely stored, and all personnel were trained on the proper use of their equipment.

Crisis Response Preparations

What All Colors did discover was that they didn't have a crisis response plan or business continuity strategies. Even though they were unlikely to experience a disruptive business crisis they were not really prepared to deal with one if it happened.

During the workshop, All Colors focused on creating a business continuity strategies document that clearly mapped the truly critical functions of the firm, the interdependencies of the tasks, and the sequence in which the tasks need to be performed in the event of a crisis.

Going into the workshop their overall risk was low but they were unprepared to react appropriately if the improbable crisis occurred—and that's what can mean survival in a fast-breaking crisis.

They learned that a low risk posture (based on a low probability of known threats and vulnerabilities) is good but the absence of a BCP is a risk in itself. They mitigated that final risk creating their plan during the workshop. Now they are ready.

FAST BUILDERS, INC.

Fast Builders, Inc. is an engineering and construction firm that employs a staff of over 100 office personnel and field supervisors to manage company equipment, two field crews of three employees and a foreman, and a large number of contractors and independent consultants.

In addition to its head office, where most of the office staff work, the company owns two small trailers that function as field offices at major construction sites.

All together the company's job sites can grow to nearly a thousand workers during construction booms. Judging by yearly revenues and the number of projects and personnel working under its aegis in an average year, it is a medium-sized business that contracts and expands as necessary to meet obligations.

Infrastructure

Its head office is located on the second (top) floor of a building that fronts a busy commercial street. The building is flat roofed and all their offices have outside-facing glass windows that are protected against storms with shutters.

To someone standing on the roof, it would look a little like a shallow pool because the building's walls rise about three feet above the rooftop itself. It has holes in many places along the bottom edge of the walls to drain rain water.

Perceived Vulnerabilities

In one incident, during uncharacteristically prolonged heavy rains, the drain holes became obstructed with leaves and other debris, and water pooled up until under pressure it found its way through cracks into the building. Unfortunately, Fast Builders was situated in the topmost floor and directly under the leaking roof, and took the brunt of the waterfall while the ground floor endured no damage.

Fast Builders suffered physical damage to computer hardware, digital data, furniture and paper file (documents and blueprints) and needed several weeks to recover only partly, and several more months to recover fully. Their revenue flow also suffered greatly but their good customer relationships, a good cash reserve, and online data backups to a cloud-based service saved them from fatal damage.

A risk assessment determined that Fast Builders' main worries are over windstorms (hurricanes), industrial accidents, fire, an active shooter/attacker or workplace violence, health hazards like asbestos or a contaminant, and regulatory compliance for worker safety. Most of these threats affect the company's own employees and those of its contractors working on the company's job sites and in their main building.

During round table discussions at the RISC/BCP workshop they came to realize they lacked an effective vendor management program to transfer the risks to their subcontractors, and to assure their performance and financial responsibility. Insurance policies alone were not enough.

Risk Management

Given their reliance on third-parties, they were concerned about operational risks and the responsibility they have for their subcontractors' negligence or failure to abide by regulations. The company undertook many steps to manage the risks. For example:

- it used a collection of management communications created over time with vendors into one vendor management manual (policy and procedures) that includes contractors' requirements for insurance, licensing, personnel screening and training, and programs for safety and regulatory compliance;

- it established a digital vendor management database to track and store each contractor's organization information and documents, like copies of licenses and insurance policies, and flags expiration dates and missing documents;

- it created the position of Chief Risk Officer (CRO) to oversee security, RISC threats (Chapter 2), the BCM program, and the vendor management program to control third-party risks;

- it charged the CRO as the plan administrator and created an emergency management committee chaired by the CRO;

- it scheduled semi-annual inspections and cleaning of its head building's roof to assure proper drainage and repair;

- it instituted quarterly *checklist tests* (page 146), and yearly *parallel tests* (page 147) that include emergency response training and drills;

- it rented an industrial park bay in an adjacent town to serve as its warm site, in which it stores its *grab kit* (page 113), backup external drive, field equipment, 2-way radios and chargers, and emergency generators; and,

- it contracted with a fuel services company to construct a fuel tank in its heavy equipment park, to deliver predefined quantities of fuel within 8 hours of notice (to power its three emergency generators and field trailers), and tied fuel delivery orders to specific early warning system (EWS) signals.

The company now practices preventive strategies, like "tenting" all electronics and other equipment and documents with plastic sheets prior to leaving the office unattended during inclement weather.

Crisis Response Preparation

Prior to the workshop Fast Builders hadn't prepared much better for a new crisis. The company's principals had a good notion of which company functions were critical but they were unorganized thoughts rather than a prioritized plan. There was no written plan for others to follow in the absence of principals directing on site. In any case, many of those thoughts would be lost under pressure in a crisis, and those they would think of would probably be acted on out of order.

Oftentimes continuity strategies are less than ideal; they are reasonable compromises. For example, this company's small but wide-ranging fleet of vehicles and heavy equipment does not merit storing in one place its own fuel for normal operations.

But fuel will be needed to run emergency generators to power its activated warm site, its field office trailers, and some select equipment for at least a week, or longer if fuel is rationed. The solution was to contract with a fuel distributor for emergency fuel supplies and to build its own fuel tank that's filled in anticipation of emergencies.

This strategy's weakness is that during a region-wide crisis fuel supplies could run out before their order is placed. A contract is useless if there is no fuel to distribute. So their emergency response is to activate its contract and order the storage tank filled as soon as the weather bureau issues a "tropical storm watch"—forecasting the possibility of a major windstorm in their area within 48 hours.

Should the anticipated emergency not lead to using the fuel, then it is kept topped until the hurricane season passes since a season can generate more than one potential wind storm. So the tank, once filled, can be kept full for the season. Once the threat passes, fuel can be used to power machinery until the tank is drained in the normal course of business.

Mitigating fast breaking crises, like fire or an active shooter, will depend on reflexive actions. Sounding an early warning or tripping an alarm to such events falls on whoever or whatever first senses the crisis. Periodic training and drills are necessary to assure people and devices respond accordingly.

Most of Fast Builders' people work as on-site construction crews but over 50 employees work in the company head office, and field hands and supervisors occasionally visit the building for administrative tasks.

Construction is an industry with high employee turnover and with many third-parties helping execute their work. Disagreements among workers and with supervisors can lead to incidents. Thus, important aspects of this company's BCP are personnel relations and management, emergency response training, drills, and vendor management for its contractors.

The company must keep a watchful eye on their people and operations and respond to early warnings to mitigate potential crises.

■   ■   ■

The most difficult aspect of producing a viable business continuity plan is the research that needs to be done before reducing the information into one succinct document.

The following chapters will guide you through the process of researching and evaluating your organization's crisis readiness, and for producing worksheets that will be the foundation of your business continuity plan.

P A R T

II

THE PROCESS

This section guides you through the research and tasks you will need to perform to understand the threats to your company, devise crisis detection indicators, and respond with feasible survival and resolution strategies.

CHAPTER

4

FIRST STEPS TO RESILIENCY

We cannot do everything at once,
but we can do something at once.

— Calvin Coolidge

STAYING IN BUSINESS through a crisis is more likely if you have done some long-range strategic planning. The basic work of identifying and articulating the truly critical from merely important (and unimportant) functions needs to be performed by everyone, from line workers to the top executives, under the direction of a skilled, neutral facilitator who will sort, weigh and blend the information. Otherwise, the task will degrade into well-meaning but misguided turf battles.

Administrative responsibilities can be controlled by the various administrative departments but the task of contingency planning must be centralized to assure that interdependencies between departments are addressed. This chapter is about easy first steps to get the project going and become resilient.

START WITH A PROJECT PLAN

A project outline for establishing a typical BCM program, shown in Figure 4.1, is provided to get you started with the creation of your own plan, and then manage and maintain it. A blank project template is also available for download as an electronic spreadsheet so you don't need to create one from scratch.

Exercise 1: Start the project with a plan for action

The creation of a BCP requires many tasks. The best way to go about this project is to cover all bases in a logical order and in minimal time by following a project plan like the example shown. Use a copy of Appendix A.1 on page 155 and just fill in the blank cells to suit your schedule. If you don't like this plan you can edit it using a downloadable spreadsheet in the quest-publishing.com website or create your own with an app or service you may already have. Note that tasks 1.1 through 1.4 are activities for this chapter.

GET MANAGEMENT BUY-IN

A company's best BCP is bound to fail in a crisis if its top leadership does not support it actively from the start. Ideally the business owner or chief executive officer (CEO) would be the program's catalyst and champion. At the very least, the head must be a willing supporter of the plan. Some of the best arguments to pose to the decision makers are that business continuity plans—

- Help avoid many risks and mitigate the unavoidable ones
- Minimize economic losses
- Reduce the probability of a crisis through awareness
- Dramatically improve recovery efforts and minimize losses
- Reduce disruptions to operations and critical functions
- Provide quick decision-making tools under time constraints

Figure 4.1: Sample business continuity project plan

TASK	TASK NAME	DURATION	START	FINISH	ASSIGNED
1	Initiate the BCM Project	4 days	3-Jan	7-Jan	Johnson
1.1	Get management buy-in	1 day	4-Jan	4-Jan	Johnson
1.2	Identify the Plan Administrator	1 day	5-Jan	6-Jan	President/CEO
1.3	Identify the Plan Creation Team	1 day	5-Jan	6-Jan	President/CEO
1.4	Communicate the plan to others	1 day	7-Jan	7-Jan	Johnson
2	Business Impact Assessment	10 days	9-Jan	20-Jan	Johnson
2.1	Review current plans	1 day	9-Jan	9-Jan	Johnson
2.2	Establish an early warning system	1 day	10-Jan	10-Jan	Sanchez
2.3	Audit the company's preparedness	1 day	11-Jan	11-Jan	Sanchez
2.4	Conduct a threat assessment	1 day	12-Jan	12-Jan	Smith
2.5	Conduct a vulnerability assessment	1 day	13-Jan	13-Jan	Gilford
2.6	Produce a cost-benefit analysis	2 days	16-Jan	17-Jan	Wiley
2.7	Identify critical business functions	2 days	18-Jan	19-Jan	Wiley
2.8	Write the BIA document	1 day	20-Jan	20-Jan	Johnson
3	Business Continuity Plan	10 days	23-Jan	3-Feb	Johnson
3.1	Position/educate plan contributors	1 day	23-Jan	23-Jan	Sanchez
3.2	Develop continuity strategies	3 days	24-Jan	26-Jan	Sanchez/Smith
3.3	Document continuity strategies	1 day	27-Jan	/27	Sanchez
3.4	Create a contact list	1 day	30-Jan	30-Jan	Smith
3.5	Produce various generic press releases	2 days	31-Jan	1-Feb	Ace Consultants
3.6	Write the BCP document	2 days	2-Feb	3-Feb	Sanchez
4	Accountability & Compliance	5 days	6-Feb	12-Feb	Johnson
4.1	Assign responsibilities to individuals	1 day	6-Feb	6-Feb	President/CEO
4.2	Establish a "Emergency Response Team"	2 days	7-Feb	8-Feb	President/CEO
4.3	Establish a "Reconstruction Team"	1 day	9-Feb	9-Feb	President/CEO
4.4	Produce a "team assignments" memo	1 day	12-Feb	12-Feb	Johnson
5	Test the Plan	8 days	19-Feb	26-Feb	Sanchez
5.1	Conduct a checklist test	1 day	19-Feb	19-Feb	Sanchez
5.2	Prepare a non-business interruption scenario	1 day	20-Feb	20-Feb	Smith
5.3	Conduct a non-business interruption test	1 day	21-Feb	21-Feb	Smith
5.4	Prepare a parallel test scenario	1 day	22-Feb	22-Feb	Sanchez
5.5	Conduct a parallel test	1 day	23-Feb	23-Feb	Sanchez
5.6	Prepare a business interruption scenario	1 day	26-Feb	26-Feb	Sanchez/Smith
5.7	Conduct a business interruption test	1 day	27-Feb	27-Feb	Sanchez/Smith
5.8	Issue a project pass/need improvement report	1 day	28-Feb	28-Feb	Johnson
6	Refine the Plan	3 days	1-Mar	3-Mar	Sanchez
6.1	Correct issues	1 day	1-Mar	1-Mar	Sanchez/Smith
6.2	Test again	1 day	2-Mar	2-Mar	Sanchez/Smith
6.3	Write a BCM program "ready" report	1 day	3-Mar	3-Mar	Johnson
7	Institute your BCM Program	1 day	4-Mar	4-Mar	President/CEO

- Segregate the truly critical functions and the unnecessary functions that needlessly consume resources and revenues
- Eliminate confusion in times of stress
- Protect assets and liabilities
- Minimize potential legal liability

- Create training materials for new employees
- Reduce insurance premiums, and
- Conform with regulatory requirements (when applicable)

In the aggregate, these are very convincing arguments, especially when each of the tasks needed to attain the benefits would be something the company should do anyway.

The BCM can be a catalyst to revenue savings and improved efficiency by identifying and ridding the organization of expired functions.

IDENTIFY THE PLAN ADMINISTRATOR

Once you have management buy-in instructions will flow down in support of the project once top management agrees with the need and value of a BCP.

Organizations are, by their very nature, composed of individuals from a variety of disciplines who act in concert to produce a product or service. An organization's success depends on the symbiotic relationships and its members' cooperation toward the group's mission.

Likewise, the success of the continuity plan will depend on the cooperation and support of members from the organization's different departments; however, part of the management

"... part of the management buy-in effort is to make one person completely responsible as the Plan Administrator ... however, all departments should participate on an advisory basis."

buy-in effort is to make one person completely responsible as the *Plan Administrator* (or a similar title) for organizing and coordinating the project during its formation and to be responsible thereafter for its ongoing maintenance.

ESTABLISH A CRISIS MANAGEMENT TEAM

If the business has more than a dozen members the plan administrator should form a crisis management team (CMT) or a plan creation team to assist him in creating a comprehensive plan. The makeup and size of the team will vary depending on the size and complexity of the organization. In most cases, one or two company members will be doing a majority of the work; but all departments should participate on an advisory basis.

In one large, exemplary company, Visa International, each department is responsible for their part, while one unit coordinates and unifies a general plan under the guidance of a consulting firm.

Using our case studies in chapter three, as small as ABC LLC

Figure 4.2: Policies that affect a business continuity plan

• Employee manuals	• Office closing policy
• Fire protection plan	• Travel policy
• Security procedures	• Evacuation plan
• Insurance plan	• Risk management plan
• Safety and health programs	• Capital improvement plan
• Data management and recovery	• Accounting procedures plan

Figure 4.3: Questions to ask your business insurance carrier

- How will your property be valued?

- Does your policy cover the cost of required upgrades to code?

- How much insurance are you required to carry to avoid becoming a coinsurer?

- What perils or causes of loss does your policy cover?

- What is your deductible?

- What does your policy require you to do in the event of loss?

- What types of records and documentation will your insurance company want to see?

- To what extent are you covered for loss due to an interruption of power? Is coverage provided for both on and off premises interruption?

- Are you covered for lost income in the event of business interruption because of a loss? How long is your coverage for lost income if the business is closed by a civil authority?

- To what extent are you covered for reduced income due to customers not all immediately coming back once business reopens?

- Will establishing a Business Continuity Plan affect your rates?

is, all it needs is a plan administrator who can just consult with the shareholders and employees of the company to conceive a BCP. Any one of the three managers could be the administrator.

All Colors, on the other hand, is large enough to consider forming a small team—possibly the senior member from each of the company's three functional sections for administration, graphics and design, and printing, plus one executive from the front office—with one of them appointed as the administrator.

Fast Builders, Inc. is another story. Its size and complexity leaves no doubt that this company needs a full-blown emergency management committee (EMC)—something more formal and typically larger than a CMT.

Whether the administrator of a very small organization produces a plan solo, or the administrator works for a sizeable, complex firm that can designate a formal committee, the same issues and topics need to be addressed.

At the very least, the units or departments performing the following functions need to be reviewed and their support enlisted by the appointed administrator:

- Senior management
- Public relations
- Communications
- Human resources
- Legal/insurance
- Information technology
- Facilities management
- Security

Figure 4.4: Organizations with emergency functions

• Chambers of commerce	• Emergency medical services organizations
• Emergency management committees	• American Red Cross
• City mayor offices	• Public works
• Fire departments	• Planning commissions
• Police departments	• Utility companies

- Purchasing
- Production
- Accounting/finance
- Sales/marketing

Individuals knowledgeable of these functions should be included in the team. Once a BCP is produced, the administrator should then form a crisis management team and specifically name the members of the CMT to establish leadership and activate the plan upon an incident.

> "CMT members should have executive authority to perform emergency functions like place material orders or activate contractual services required to execute the BCP, without needing a higher approval."

Where an EMC is tasked with producing policy, procedures and crisis preparatory materials in the calm of normal times—the BCM program that includes a BCP—the CMT kicks into gear to execute the BCP when an early warning alert is triggered.

The crisis management team should include members *empowered* to immediately deal with media inquiries, assess damage, begin restoration of data from off-sites, trigger a move to an alternate site, and repair damaged systems.

CMT members should have executive authority to perform emergency functions like place material orders or activate contractual services required to execute the BCP, without needing a higher approval.

Realistic time frames should be established for both the completion of each action item and the overall project. The person assigned to each action item will be in charge of managing her task according to an overall project plan.

Our BCP project plan illustrated in Figure 4.1 on page 61 can serve as a model to kick start your BCP project and manage task assignments.

REVIEW CURRENT PLANS AND POLICIES

Certain easily deployed preventative measures can be taken to lessen the blow of a disaster. Start with a review of internal policies and procedures (Figure 4.2) to determine if any measures are already in place.

While reviewing these policies, keep in mind the critical products, services, and operations your business depends on daily. It is important to identify these elements and make arrangements in your recovery planning to have them reestablished immediately. There are three areas to assess:

- Products and services along with the facilities and equipment needed to produce them
- Products and services provided by suppliers (especially sole-source providers)
- Operations, equipment, and personnel vital to the continued functioning of the facility

A common flaw in disaster recovery plans is the oversight of adequate insurance. Since insurance companies often sell pre-set packages, it is not until a disaster strikes that most businesses realize they are not properly insured.

Without good planning, inappropriate insurance coverage becomes evident during a disaster, when it can be most devastating. The importance of reviewing your coverage with your provider

(Figure 4.3 on page 64) as part of your BCP to determine your business' changing insurance needs cannot be overstated.

Another essential step of the planning process is to take into account the resources that will be provided by local government agencies, utilities, and community organizations in the event of a disaster (Figure 4.4 on page 65).

You may be able to plan for their services in your recovery plan. In developing your plan, ask yourself this question: What services will the city or county provide in case of different emergencies that can affect my business?

COMMUNICATE THE PROJECT

Effective communications with company personnel is all important in conducting a risk assessment. Their responses to your questions depend on their perception of your intent. Its also important that individuals assess accurately what functions they can and cannot do without, and for how long. Their recovery time estimates under normal conditions can vary wildly from their actual needs during an emergency.

Another factor that alters the perception of recovery time is when a function is evaluated independently when in fact it is not independent. The loss of an interdependent function is likely to have a cascading effect on other functions.

Sensitizing participants beforehand to put themselves in a *survival* mindset rather than *business as usual* is also important so realistic, cost-effective measures can be identified during the planning process (Barr, 2002).

Tell Others Why You Need a Continuity Plan

An assessment of your organization's activities will help you evaluate the risk of business process failures and help identify critical and necessary functions and their resource dependencies.

You can communicate to the members of the "plan creation team" (who may be the same people who comprise the crisis management team) that the risk assessment does several things:

- Provides an independent and interdependent view of risks
- Provides a basis for determining cost-effective strategies
- Determines critical and necessary business functions and processes and their resource dependencies
- Identifies critical computer applications and the associated outage tolerance
- Determines the impact upon market share and image
- Identifies regulatory/compliance exposure
- Estimates the financial and operational impact of the disruption and the required recovery time objective (RTO)

Set Recovery Time Objectives

The RTO is the amount of time allowed for recovery of a business function. If exceeded, severe damage to the organization results. Time and dollar estimates allow management to make an informed decision on how to allocate recovery funds. Finally, an assessment allows information technology services to determine RTOs for applications that support critical business units.

Initiate Data Collection

Once you have identified the plan administrator, you have gotten management buy-in, and you have identified the members of the plan creation team (and they may the same as the crisis management team), you are ready to inform the company of it.

Exercise 2: Distribute business continuity surveys
One way to announce the BCP project is through a written request to the other participants for their input. It could be a memoran-

Figure 4.5: Business continuity survey example

CONTINUITY STRATEGIES SURVEY

Name: Helen Gordon

Title: Vice President

Department: Media, Marketing & Sales

This survey is to identify the absolutely critical functions that your section/department/company must perform within 3 days in order to survive. Such functions contribute directly to the organization's bottom line and without which the organization's survival is questionable. Typically, such functions include production, client relations, cash flow operations, etc. Please complete the following sections in preparation/update of our company business continuity plan (BCP). Use the following scale to rate criticality matters.

CRITICALITY SCALE	Comments
1 = Most Critical	needed immediately; cannot function without it
2 = Highly Critical	cannot disrupt longer than 24 hours without risking the company
3 = Critical	cannot disrupt longer than 3 days without risking the company
4 = Secondary	disruption past 2 week(s) would hurt operations
5 = Non-critical	disruption would be an inconvenience but would not risk the company

Criticality of Functions

For all applicable, use the criticality scale to rate the functions you perform for the following:

N/A	Billing (accounts receivable)	N/A	Billing (accounts payable)
4	Job scheduling	N/A	Job execution
N/A	Shipping	3	Customer service
2	Order processing	N/A	Payroll
1	Media relations		

Tasks Associated to Applicable Functions

Lists any tasks that **need** to be performed in support of the critical functions listed above. Also list any equipment, forms or communications devices needed to perform the tasks.

▷ Research calls (need either paper notepads/pens or 2 charged notebook PCs)

▷ In-person interviews of clients, employees, vendors and others (POVs for transport)

▷ Liaison calls/fax to media for press releases (2 alternate voice comm. devices)

▷ Six 25"x30" sticky easel pads, 1 easel, colored markers, large erasable wall calendar

▷

Page 1 of 2

dum covering a copy of "Appendix A.2: Business Continuity Survey" on page 156. You may also want to attach copies of "Figure 4.6: Examples of business continuity strategies" on page

Business continuity survey example (continued)

Existing Replacement Arrangements (to replace existing systems or equipment or supplies)

▷ Satellite telephone service

▷ Alternate Internet service provider

▷ Wireless connection (cell. phones with hotspot)

Essential Operating Procedures (needed to maintain an efficient work flow)

▷ Research accounts and procedures, inc. passwords, etc.

▷ Employee handbook

▷ Burden and bill rates schedules, etc.

Equipment or Supplies for Off-Site Storage

▷ Two (2) notebook computers

▷ Two (2) laptop battery chargers

▷ Portable/mobile printer

Vital Records (those that are uniquely valuable in your purview)

▷ Company checks

▷ Client and vendor contracts

▷ Insurance policies/contracrts, etc.

Back-up Procedures (for servers, desktop/notebook computers in your purview)

▷ Back-up tapes and hard disk stored off-site

▷ Hard copy of clients' projects (and cases)

▷ Hard copy of manuals, templates, etc.

Temporary Operating Procedures (in the event your office facility becomes unavailable)

▷ Move main operations to alternate (warm) site

▷ Let clients and vendors know the circumstances, and alternate phone/contacts

▷ Update/notify the emergency status as needed to employees and clients

▷ Scheduling and planning from activated warm site

▷ Except for VP/director, employees may temporarily have to work from home

▷ If available, comm. by phones; if not available, comm by daily courier run or radio)

2 of 2

72 to the survey to give participants ideas and guidance about what goes into the survey. Business continuity strategies are discussed is greater detail in page 97.

Figure 4.6: Examples of business continuity strategies

Accounts Payable
- Match receiving reports to invoices manually.
- Selectively approve invoices with large discounts.
- Defer other payments until computer processing capability is restored.

Accounts Receivable
- Prepare a "short list" of problem credit accounts; manually analyze and approve credit.
- Automatically approve other orders from existing customers up to a specified limit.
- Approve new customer orders manually.
- Apply cash after computer processing capability is restored.

Billing
- Invoice large dollar amounts manually.
- Defer other invoicing until computer processing capability is restored.

Cost Accounting
- Collect raw cost accounting data manually.
- Prepare cost accounting reports after computer processing capability is restored.

Customer Service
- Refer to the latest hard copy of job status.
- Explain to customers that the computer system is down, but that you will check the status of their orders and call them back.

- Use standard production times for standard products and consult experienced process control personnel for estimated delivery times for special orders.

Engineering
- Use aperture cards to view engineering change orders.
- Process changes manually that will have an impact on work-in-progress.
- Implement critical work-in-process changes manually.

Fixed Assets
- Maintain a manual log of transactions during the interim processing period.
- Update records and prepare reports when computer processing capability is restored.

General Ledger
- Obtain copies of the most recent financial statements.
- If an outage occurs during the closing cycle, use top-line estimates to close the books or defer closing until computer processing capability is restored.

Human Resources
- Defer employee status and salary changes until computer processing capability is restored.
- Make retrospective salary adjustments after computer processing capability is restored.

Examples of business continuity strategies (continued)

Inventory Management
- Use a computer service bureau to print a copy of prior day's computer record of inventory status.
- Intentionally over-order "B" and "C" items to prevent stockouts. Work off excess inventory later.
- Monitor and reorder "A" items manually.
- Update computer records for transactions during the stabilization period.

Material Requirements Planning
- Operate using the latest hard copy master schedule, adjust manually.
- Intentionally over-order "B" and "C" items with the expectation of working off excess inventory later.
- Manually review impact of new requirements/changes, and selectively order additional "A" items as deemed necessary.
- Manually review impact of new requirements/changes, and selectively order additional "A" items as deemed necessary.

Order Processing
- Use fax or phone to receive electronic data interchange (EDI) orders.
- Write new orders manually.
- Prepare copies for order picking or production scheduling.
- Copy and mark up previous orders to use for future similar orders.
- Use latest copy of order status combined with actual shop floor visits to update work-in-progress status.

Payroll
- Obtain the latest copy of payroll check images and use a local computer utility to produce duplicate copies.
- Store the most recent backup copy of check images off site.
- Manually prepare checks for new hires and remove checks for terminations.
- Include a notice with payroll checks indicating that shortages or overages will be corrected upon normalcy.

Production Scheduling
- Obtain the latest hard copy of the master schedule and the detailed production schedule.
- Prepare move tickets manually as needed.
- Manually update latest production schedule.

Purchasing
- Update the latest hard copy of material status manually.
- Prepare copis of purchse orders for receiving.
- Expedite manually.

Receiving
- If necessary, use "no P.O." (purchase order) procedures to receive material.
- Use a copy of the packing list to document receipt.
- Record receipts manually on a backup form.
- Send a copy of each receipt form to accounts payable for approval of invoices.

Shipping
- Prepare bills of lading manually.
- Use similar prior shipment records to develop routing.

If you are the only person producing the BCP this exercise will put you in the necessary frame of mind to continue. If others are assisting with the project they can mull over the surveys while you go on with other tasks. You will use the information in the completed forms during exercises in Chapters 5, 6 and 7.

Very small companies can involve everyone in the creation of the plan. Larger organizations usually only involve representatives from each of the departments. Regardless of the number of people the plan administrator recruits into the plan creation team, they are likely to seek information and documents from others in their departments.

■   ■   ■

Now that you have gotten your organization committed to preparing for emergencies, you are ready to begin your research and start creating the various components of your crisis parachute—the pilot chute (threat and risk assessment), the canopy (risk mitigation strategies), the shroud lines (crisis response actions), the harness (business continuity strategies), and the ripcord (your early warning system)—to let you down safely when you have to manage a budding or exploding crisis.

C H A P T E R

5

KNOW YOUR CRISES

What we anticipate seldom occurs;
what we least expect generally happens.

—Benjamin Disraeli

TO MANAGE RISKS you need to "know" what the potential threats are and avoid surprises by arming your organization with tools and strategies that will cushion the blows of a crisis.

Remember, though, that such a program needs to be well-conceived and practiced beforehand to render the expected results when events turn sour. Impromptu strategies during a crisis may not work, or they may yield unexpected outcomes.

The threats to worry about most are the ones you don't know or mitigate. You should constantly scan your business horizon. New threats can sneak up on the organization by being seemingly unimportant or irrelevant—until they happen.

This chapter deals with the various actions you can take to identify and mitigate the risks that can face your organization.

IDENTIFY AND ASSESS RISKS

In this book we offer a simple way to catalog and rank risks. This methodology is meant for small businesses who handle their own security and emergency preparations.

To conduct a threat assessment you need to establish the probability of a disaster due to one or more threats, determine how vulnerable the business is to each threat, and determine what the potential impact each threat would have if it happened. These can be calculated with a simple formula.

Elements of a Risk Assessment Formula

The U.S. Department of Homeland Security (DHS) currently uses the following formula for its assessments of national infrastructures and issues of public safety:

$$T * V * C = R$$

where "T" is Threat, "V" is Vulnerability, "C" is Consequence, and "R" is Risk. This is the essence of the DHS' formula although in practice the formula takes on a variety of sub factors and complex calculations.

Since many public agencies and private practitioners have

You should constantly scan your business horizon. New threats can sneak up on the organization by being seemingly unimportant or irrelevant—until they happen.

---

adopted DHS's formula, so have we; but you will see that we use the term "impact" synonymously with "consequence," as in "business impact assessment, or BIA."

Threats are potential hazards that, should they materialize, can disrupt an organization's operations, or even push it to the point of failure. We measure (rate) threats on a simple numerical scale to determine their probability of happening.

Table 5.1: Threat probability criteria

Rating	Description
1	Unlikely or very unlikely to occur
2	Could occur - moderate chance of occurrence
3	Likely or very likely to occur

Vulnerability is the degree of exposure to threats. An organization's vulnerability can be mitigated through internal ("i") or external ("e") resources. You control internal resources through your funds, facilities, equipment, people or contracts. External resources are those you count on to be provided by others, like police or fire/rescue services.

Table 5.2: Vulnerability criteria

Rating	Description
1	Well mitigated
2	Adequately mitigated
3	Poorly mitigated or not mitigated

Consequence (impact) is the factor that measures the degree of disruption such a crisis would cause the business. A crisis can affect just one, or two, or all three areas that make an organization viable: its business functions ("f"), its assets ("a"), and its people ("p"). These are the three sub factors that are critical to keeping a business functioning during a crisis.

When measuring impact, consider the company's recovery time objectives (RTO) discussed in the last chapter on page 69.

Table 5.3: Consequence/impact criteria

Rating	Description
1	No discernible impact on business, assets or people
2	Negative but surmountable effects on operations, assets or people
3	Could disrupt or paralyze operations or hamper output

Risk is the mathematical product of the rated variables. The score for the listed threats can be compared to identify the company's greatest weaknesses and prioritize their mitigation.

Let's take this information and rewrite the basic $T * V * C = R$ formula into our working model. We supplant vulnerability (V) with the sum of its sub variables of i+e, and we supplant consequence (C) with the sum of its sub variables of f+a+p to produce the following working formula:

$$T * (i + e) * (f + a + p) = R$$

This formula is reflected in the table header of the worksheets we provide for risk assessments in Appendix A.3 and Figure 5.1.

Applying Values to the Formula

Assigning values is a subjective business. What's important is that the assessor, or the assessment team, apply the criteria as evenly as possible so the outcome for the set of threats is not skewed. Your goal is to compare apples with apples.

Mistakenly underestimating or exaggerating your parameters for low, moderate or high risk is not as important as applying them consistently so that potential risks can be prioritized effectively. If you find that too many risks turn out to be assessed as

Figure 5.1: Risk assessment worksheet example

Threat	Prob. X	Vulnerability		X		Consequence			= RISK
		Int. + Ext. = Sum			Business+ Assets + People = Sum Functions /Prop.				
Hurricane or flooding	2	2	3	5	3	3	2	8	80
Fire due to stored paper and printing chemicals	2	3	1	4	3	3	3	9	72
Printing equipment break	2	2	2	4	2	1	1	4	32
Data loss/corruption	2	1	1	2	3	1	1	5	20
Communications loss	1	1	2	3	2	1	1	4	12
Loss of key officer	2	1	1	2	2	1	1	4	16
Loss of key employee(s)	1	3	1	3	2	1	2	5	15
Reputational damage	1	1	1	2	1	1	1	3	6
Criminal/terrorist attack	1	3	1	4	3	2	3	8	32
Lawsuit (EEO, disorim.)	1	1	1	2	1	2	2	5	10
Loss of key client	2	1	2	3	1	2	1	4	24

LEGEND:
Prob. = probability of occuring
Int. = internal resources
Ext. = external resources

Threat Probability Criteria:
1 Unlikely to occur
2 Could occur (moderate)
3 Likely to occur

Vulnerability Criteria:
1 Well mitigated (through assets, personnel, vendors and/or procedures)
2 Adequately mitigated (good but for minor weakness/issue)
3 Poorly mitigated or not mitigated (an important weakness remains)

Consequence Criteria:
1 No discernable impact on business, assets or people
2 Negative but surmountable effects on operations, assets or people
3 Potentially disrupts or paralyzes operations and hampers output

Ranges: 5 to 30 = low risk | 31 to 55 = moderate risk | 56 to 80 = high risk | 81+ = dangerous weakness

high you can adjust your definitions to be more stringent.

To use this formula refer to the legend in the grey box of Figure 5.1, and follow our logic for applying values to a new wind storm threat in the following hypothetical scenario:

- If your business is situated in a "hurricane alley" and the threat of a major wind storm is *likely* to occur (T=3); and,

- the business' building is *unprotected* against high winds and you *cannot* count on external services (like fire/rescue) for help in the midst of the storm (V=3+3=6); and

- it would be likely that the facility and its contents would be *trashed* and your employees would be *out of work* while your operations stopped for weeks to rebuild (C=3+3+3=9);

then this threat would be calculated as 3 * 6 * 9 = 162, the highest risk any threat could be scored because everything is the worst.

In reality, though, hardly any threat merits such extreme ratings—threes across the board. You probably would not rate the probability as likely to occur unless the threat were a strong possibility or imminent.

Consider our All Colors Printing Company example on page 50 for a more realistic calculation during the planning phase when the hurricane threat is a possibility but not an active one:

- Here you would consider that a major wind storm could pass your way (T=2) if you're in "hurricane alley"; and

- you believe that the see-through brick wall fronting the glass storefront provides adequate protection from flying debris (i=2) but you will not be able to count on external services because outside resources will not respond during a hurricane (e=3); and

- as a consequence you'd stop functioning for days if not weeks (f=3), important equipment could be damaged (a=3), and your people's availability for work would likely be affected for some time (p=2).

Figure 5.2: Types of crises that could affect your business

• Fires, explosions and other industrial accidents	• Terrorism (assaults, bombings, biological agents)
• Severe weather (hurricanes, tornados, windstorms, blizzards, floods, etc.	• Crime (robbery, embezzlement, fraud, workplace violence by employee or intruder)
• Health issues (contagions, poisoning, sanitation, pollution)	• Theft of key trade secrets or intellectual property
• Technological emergencies (telecom failure, computer failure, data corruption	• Lawsuits or criminal proceedings
	• Regulatory changes or challenges
• Facility problems (poor construction or condition)	• Industrial accidents
• Cooling system failure	• Labor strikes
• Utility/energy/power outage	• Product tampering
• Transportation accident	• Loss of key officers, leaders, or customers
• Hazardous materials mishandling	• Personnel issues (carelessness, misconduct)

Given this reasoning during planning, a realistic calculation for this scenario would be 2*(2+3)*(3+3+2)=80. That's a very high risk score. In fact, it's practically *dangerous*, per our scale.

What kind of threat would merit a 3 probability? Here is one clear example: If you run a convenience store in a crime-ridden neighborhood and the neighborhood has experienced robberies it's likely your store will be targeted for a robbery.

After you have listed the threats you will need to consider your vulnerabilities. Expect that the crisis will affect many more businesses than yours. For instance, data corruption due to a viral outbreak will likely affect many businesses at once. Worse, a catastrophic energy failure could black out an entire region for days or weeks where your business is.

So, apply the following questions for each threat as you assess vulnerabilty:

- If you depend on internal resources, will your staff be practiced and competent enough to resolve the threat within the RTO if the issue is new and fixes are not yet known?

- If you depend on external resources, will outside technical consultants or help lines be available to help resolve the problem within your stated recovery time objective (RTO)?

- Finally, will external resources respond to your business' needs in a timely manner? Or will the needs of others take precedence?

When considering consequences, business horizons vary according to industry and your particular business model. A web-based technology firm may consider its short-, mid- and long-term horizons to be four hours, three months and one year.

On the other hand an established heavy equipment manufacturer is likely to have far longer horizons; perhaps a week, one year and five years for its short-, mid- and long-term horizons, because it is a far more mature industry and its product delivery schedules are not so sensitive to momentary pressures and impatient clients.

Table 5.4: Suggested scoring chart

5 to 30	=	a **low risk** overall that does not require special attention
31 to 55	=	a **moderate risk** issue that should be mitigated
56 to 80	=	a **high risk** issue that needs priority mitigation
81 up	=	a **dangerous** weakness that needs to be mitigated ASAP

While a manufacturing plant could probably survive a weeks-long supply-chain disruption, such an event could drive a fast-breaking information technology firm to lose its customer base and into financial insolvency.

This exercise, the production of a risk assessment, is meant to identify no more than three or four high risk threats to focus on until they are mitigated. Then you can choose to address the next worst threat from the moderate ones on your list if you want.

An average moderate score using this worksheet is 48. That's the product of all factors and sub factors set to a 2 rating $(2*[2+2]*[2+2+2]=48)$, and we already know that the absolute highest score here can be 162 when every variable is set to 3. Given this, you could use Table 5.4 to prioritize your remedial actions, or set your own parameters.

Using our suggested system, threats that score 81 or higher should receive your undivided attention. Some administrators

Figure 5.3: Risk mitigation strategies

- Develop additional emergency procedures
- Conduct additional training
- Acquire additional equipment
- Establish mutual aid agreements with other organizations
- Establish preferential service agreements with vendors, like emergency office space

Figure 5.4: Risk mitigation strategies worksheet example

Type of Risk	Action or Product	Source	Action by
Wind storm protect	Install hurricane shutters	Shield Awnings	8/20/XX
Wind storm protect	Procure large plastic "tenting"	Abe's Hardware	8/20/XX
Wind storm protect	Inspect roof, seal, clear of debris	Hardy Roofs	8/2/XX
Fire	Relocate chemicals/flamables to detatched outside storage	John/Judy	5/30/XX
Fire	Purchase 3 more extinguishers	John	5/30/XX
Fire	Install new sprinkler system	Mike Alarms	6/30/XX
Fire	Produce bldg. emergency plan	Judy	7/1/XX
Printing equip.	Upgrade to "priority" service acct	IBM Co.	6/30XX
Criminal/terrorism	Front reception panic button	Mike Alarms	6/30/XX
Criminal/terrorism	Write crisis response procedure	CEO Smith	6/30/XX
Criminal/terrorism	Give crisis response training	Judy	7/15/XX
Loss of key officer	Cross-train EVP ASAP	CEO Smith	2/15/XX
Loss of key officer	Hire new V.P. ASAP and train	CEO Smith	12/30/XX
Loss of key officer	BOP insurance policy	Ace Ins. Co.	6/1/XX
Loss of key client	Diversify services and get more clients	CEO Smith	8/30/XX
Image/reputation	Liaison with town gazette	Cynthia	5/30/XX
Image/reputation	Liaison with Fla. Bus. Journal	Cynthia	5/30/XX
Image/reputation	Join GMCC and participate	CEO Smith	6/1/XX
Image/reputation	Join Jax CC and participate	Julia	6/1/XX

may set different thresholds. For example, you could designate a score of 56 or higher as a disruptive crisis in the making.

The threshold scores you choose will probably depend on the number of crises that could affect your business. If your business' full list consists of only four or five threats that could affect the business, you may choose to address any threat that scores above 30 if you have the time and resources. But if your list of potential issues is long, say 10 to 15 of them, then you'll want to focus on a handful—the worst. Preparing for those will set the stage for dealing with lesser problems as well.

Exercise 3: Produce a risk assessment

Now that we have a handle on the variables that go into a risk assessment, let's produce yours.

Although it's not all inclusive, the list of generic crises shown in Figure 5.2 may help you recognize some of the threats that could apply to your business.

Use a blank worksheet (Appendix A.3 on page 158) to list the threats to your business in the left column as illustrated in Figure 5.1. This example is for the "All Colors Printing Company" on page 48. Yours will be different, of course.

Risk assessment forms and spreadsheets that calculate entries automatically can be downloaded from quest-publishing.com.

RISK MITIGATION STRATEGIES

Once you have assessed the threats and your vulnerabilities you can turn to the task of determining your ability to correct or mitigate them.

Exercise 4: Identify your risk mitigation strategies

Figure 5.3 provides some ideas for strategies that are commonly used to mitigate risks, and Figure 5.4 is an example of a completed risk mitigation strategies worksheet.

To create yours, use a blank worksheet (Appendix A.4 on page 159) to identify your organization's strategies while keeping the following questions in mind:

- Do you have the internal resources and capabilities needed?

- If you do not have the resources internally, are they available externally?

- Will external resources respond to your business' needs in a timely manner or will the needs of others take precedence?

Answer them with the following worst case scenario in mind: *the expected crisis would affect many more businesses than yours.*

For instance, data corruption due to a viral outbreak will likely affect many businesses at once. If you depend on external resources, will outside technical consultants or help lines be available to help resolve the problem within the stated recovery time objective (RTO)? And if you depend on internal resources, will your staff be practiced and competent enough to resolve such an issue within the RTO if the computer virus is new and fixes are not yet known?

Review the results of your assessment and take immediate steps to minimize vulnerabilities due to inefficient operations, inadequate systems or facility maintenance, poor data backup practices, clear safety hazards, on-site storage of vital documents, etc. By correcting obvious problems, you will reduce your vulnerability and immediately minimize your exposure.

In choosing an external resource remember to keep distances or other separations so that the calamity that affects you is unlikely to affect your external resource. This is a common problem that blind-sides many businesses at the worst of times.

Having scored your risk to the identified threats, you can now make choices to manage the risks. The following five frequently cited techniques provide you with risk management options:

Avoid risk by not performing dangerous activities. You may want to outsource processes that are hazardous to health or premises. In one example, some medical doctors desist from risky medical practices such as surgery. In the investigative profession, an investigator may forego certain techniques that risk public complaints or may be misinterpreted as harassment.

Reduce risk by taking preventive measures like installing surveillance equipment or handrails, access controls, or implementing new policies and training for visitors, your field workers, delivery drivers, or clinical technicians and similar personnel. Taking such measures may also result in lowered insurance premiums.

Assume risk through higher insurance deductibles or by determining through a cost-benefit analysis (see an example in page 103) that evaluates if the front-end payout (insurance premiums) or preventive equipment purchase) outweighs the cost of potential consequences.

Transfer risk by contract by getting others to assume responsibility for liability claims through a contract, as a tenant or employee may be required to do. For example, you may institute a policy to compensate your sales force for work-related private vehicle mileage in return for an agreement that it is their responsibility to insure that their personal automobile insurance policies cover work-related travel. You could go one step further and also require that they provide the business with copies of their policies showing the required coverage.

Transfer risk through insurance by seeking an insurance policy to absorb the costs of a crisis or business interruption or other business hazards in exchange for a premium (Wisconsin 2003; New York 2004). The more popular insurance coverages for small businesses are:

- Property
- Liability
- Business interruption
- Workers compensation
- Excess liability, or "umbrella" policy
- Employment practices liability
- Officers' and directors' liability
- Office at home
- Key person

- Professional liability
- Business owner's polity (BOP), or all-in-one

Another type of insurance—kidnap and ransom—is seldom talked about but necessary for international companies and individuals who frequently work or reside in countries where kidnapping is a criminal industry or a political hazard. "K&R insurance" coverage is particularly important for traveling executives and personnel posted in high risk areas of the world.

Poor economies motivate criminal kidnappings, and politics motivate terrorist kidnappings. To make matters worse, relying on local law enforcement to resolve such crises is oftentimes unwise either because they may not be competent crisis negotiators or investigators or police elements may even be involved in the schemes, or both.

The next step in analyzing your risk is determining whether to accept or correct the other threats that are more costly to rectify.

In presenting the risks to senior management, it is important that management knows what the risks are, what their probable consequences are, and what steps can be taken to avoid or minimize them.

One of the best ways of providing this information to management is through an effective cost-benefit analysis, which we will discuss further on.

EARLY WARNING SYSTEM

Averting a crisis can be accomplished by detecting the warning signs early on while a crisis is incipient and not full blown.

Of course, a business' early warning system (EWS) is not like the complex, electronic detection systems of the U.S. military. Still, many businesses, like energy companies and computer infrastructure providers, use mechanical or technological means to monitor the performance of sophisticated systems.

In late Summer of 2003 a simple failure in one power relay station in Ohio went uncorrected and quickly triggered a cascade of power failures that blacked out the Northeast quadrant of the United States and Canada.

The blooming failure was detected but signs (on power grid monitor gauges) were not interpreted correctly while the crisis could still be localized and mitigated.

This was a failure in the power company's early warning system.

Figure 5.5: Non-technical early warning sources and signals

TYPE OF RISK	SOURCE (WHAT TO MONITOR)	SIGNAL (ALARMING EVENT)	IMMEDIATE RESPONSE
Loss of key officer	Health checkups	Medical illness or condition	Treatment, notify BOP insurance company
Loss of key client	Customer survey by mgt.	Client complaint, comment	Apologize and resolve
Loss of key employee	Health checkups	Medical illness or condition	Treatment
Loss of key employee	Employee performance	Absenteeism, tardiness	Establish correct cause, counsel, assist
Proprietary info. loss	Customer lists, surveys	Customer defections, emp. left for competitor	Investigate why customers switched
Data loss or corruption	Computer performance	Erratic behavior, slow operation	Backup, run anti-virus, repair hardware, reinstall software
Data loss or corruption	Backup tapes	Corrupted/blank	Repair drive and/or cloud DB connection
Network failure	Connection performance	Interrupted connection	Call IT to repair
Production equipment	Operating smoothness	Unusual sounds	Call technician for inspection/repair
Image/ reputation	Media clipping service	Unfavorable article	Research; correct; issue press release
Internal theft	Inventory	Missing inventory	Investigation

It was caused not by a lack of signals but by human error. Better training could have avoided this crisis before the dominos fell.

Your organization probably isn't as dependent on machinery and electronics, but warning signals will still be there. It's up to you to have identified them and have learned to interpret them in anticipation of a crisis.

The simpler the system is the better because warning signals will be clearer and easier to monitor. Stick to real indicators for

Figure 5.6: Early warning system worksheet example

Risk Description	Source (what to monitor)	Signal (alarming event)
Hurricane or flooding	Weather channel report	Good poss. of strike in days
Hurricane or flooding	Weather channel report	In poss. Storm path next day
Fire due to stored chem.	Storage area inspections	Liquid puddle in storage shed
Fire hazards	Smoke alarm	Alarm activates
Loss of a key officer	Medical exams	Failed exam
Loss of a key officer	Medical exams	Medical condition
Image/reputation injury	News media	Negative coverage
Image/reputation injury	Client satisfaction surveys	Negative responses
Communications loss	Telephone connection	Service interruptions
Communications loss	Internet connection	Service interruptions
Lawsuits	Client satisfaction surveys	Legal complaint
Lawsuits	Employee workplace reviews	Personnel complaint
Loss of key employee	Personnel file periodic reviews	Dropping productivity
Loss of key employee	Personnel file periodic reviews	Potential of resignations
Loss of key client	Written/verbal communication	Call re. project lateness
Loss of a key client	Written/verbal communication	Complaint call

critical functions.

But, what can serve as signals in your organization if you don't rely on sophisticated electronics and gages? We'll cover that in the next exercise.

Exercise 5: Create an early warning system

Having identified the threats to your company, complete an EWS worksheet (Appendix A.5 on page 160) to create a warning system for your company.

mediate Response	Monitor
tivate 48-hour prep. plan	President
tivate 24-hour prep. plan	President
cure/inspect/remedy or rt	Admin.
acuate / confirm/ call 911	Admin.
ternate K.O. cross-training	EVP
ternate K.O. cross-training	EVP
planatory news release/ medial plan announcement	President
rrect perceived wrong / form clients	Marketing Director
itch to alternate account	President
itch to wireless hotspot	Admin.
dit, then settle or challenge	Legal
dit, then remedy if valid	Legal
erview, counsel/assist	EVP
view opportunities/benefits/ rkplace conditions/ pervision	EVP
sh to highest ority/resolve	Proj. Mgr.
sonal attention/remedy	President

Figure 5.6 is an example of a completed early warning system. Review the work tools you use to run your organization to find "things" that can serve as your "canaries in a coal mine."

Examples of non-technical/non-mechanical early warning sources and signals are shown in Figure 5.5. Unlike mechanical gauges, digital indicators, or alarms, such "soft" sources of signals are harder to recognize and formulate responses for.

Although some may be applicable to you, give thought to what warning signs are particular to your company and industry.

Once you have identified them for your business,

the next step is to determine what source will emit the signal and, most importantly, charge someone to monitor each source.

MEDIA RELATIONS BEFORE A CRISIS

Exxon learned about the importance of media relations when in 1989 the oil spill occurred in the pristine Alaskan waters of Prince William Sound. The mishandling of that incident cost the company far more than the expense of clean up operations. Exxon management's reticence to deal with the media openly only prolonged its villainous image cast by the media and bred public hostility toward the company.

The damage to its reputation left its employees demoralized even after more than a decade after the incident, and it continues to be cited as a classical case of crisis mismanagement. Many say that the environment recovered better than Exxon.

An ongoing relationship with the media is imperative for many businesses, large and small. Companies need not be international conglomerates like Exxon to benefit from good media relations. Nor does a company need a media relations department to deal with the media.

Two simpler media-related risk management strategies are available: first, the principal of a small firm can draft stand-by press releases for each of the crises that realistically could impair the company; or, second, the company can outsource this work to a public relations (PR) firm with established media and public relations channels.

Think of preemptive PR work as an insurance policy. It may cost some money. At first it may appear to be of no immediate value; but the chief executive officer or contracted PR firm should be fostering good will for the company among its media channels even in good times.

Every good deed or success should be heralded in some corner of the media's business section. The repetition of good news garners "credits" for the company for that potential rainy day.

A side benefit of an ongoing PR campaign—before a crisis happens—is that it is also good marketing and it can increase cash flow to offset the cost of PR. Whether its executives run it themselves or outsource it, companies should not forego the establishment of a good media and public relations program any more than they would operate without insurance.

Regardless of its size, a company should have at least one person generating good will through its local newspapers and stations.

A company exists to interact commercially with the community it serves. That alone is reason enough to establish a positive image building program for community involvement with chambers of commerce, local civic groups (for youths, seniors, crime

---

> "A side benefit of an ongoing PR campaign—before a crisis happens—is that it is also good marketing and it can increase cash flow to offset the cost of PR. ... [C]ompanies should not forego the establishment of a good media and public relations program any more than they would operate without insurance."

---

watch committees, etc.) or a church. Any one of these venues can present potential media exposure and contacts. They also present marketing opportunities.

No company business continuity plan or program should neglect the importance of media and public relations. Make sure that your plan clearly considers its options and pre-emptive strategies for dealing with the media before a crisis occurs, and include this in your risk mitigation and crisis response strategies.

Finally, if you cannot think of the names of at least two media representatives for your contact list (who cover your company's territory) you may end up short in the containment phase of a crisis.

Your local media representatives are likely to be syndicated with a national conglomerate like Reuters and can be your friendly channel during a crisis. Positive or negative coverage begins with your local reporters.

Establishing good media relations is a very important step in the creation of a business continuity program, what follows the plan. This step is a project in itself so an exercise for establishing good media relations is not included in this book. But don't skip the media relations efforts on a continuing basis.

■   ■   ■

Your planning up to this point has been to identify and preempt the potential crises your company may have to face. At this point you are ready to consider what you will have to do and have in place to survive the crises you cannot prevent.

CHAPTER

6

PREPARATIONS FOR A FALL

*There's no harm in hoping for the best
as long as you're prepared for the worst.*

— Stephen King,
"Different Seasons"

N O MATTER HOW well a company prepares for the worst, crises can still happen. Prior planning and mitigating, as you may have done in the previous chapter, will avoid most threats. But some will manifest anyway, and the difference between successfully managing a crisis and failure lies in the continuity strategies your organization devised and instituted beforehand.

This chapter guides you through two steps that aim to prepare you for the crisis you cannot avoid: identifying the company's critical functions the organization *must* perform to stay "alive" through a crisis; and then devise alternate systems or methods that will permit operational continuation even if a crisis incapacitates your primary systems.

PLANNING FOR A "STORMY DAY"

In the last chapter you identified potential threats to your organization. Now you need to develop alternate strategies for when a threat materializes; strategies that describe how essential business functions will continue until lost work space, technologies or processes are restored.

Alternate strategies reflect alternate management practices that (a) department heads are willing to invoke for a short period of time, (b) constitute an acceptable amount of temporary efficiency loss, and (c) focus only on business functions that have a direct bearing on either cash flow or customer service.

Asking individual departments to document their own strategies may seem logical but continuity and compatibility between departments or activities need to be coordinated. Department managers should be the architects of "what if" strategies but one individual, the Plan Administrator, should control the documentation process.

Once you've listed what really must be done—the critical functions—you'll also know what to collect for the emergency "grab kit" that's covered in the next chapter: what paper forms, reports, crucial documents and equipment you'll need to support the strategies.

Without this list you're certain to miss critical functions and you won't have the tools needed to implement them. This is not something to do in the crush of a crisis.

The business continuity strategies shown in Figure 4.6 on page 72 are good examples of what your company should think through while your heads are clear and time is on your side.

In this chapter we'll cover tools you can use to formulate business continuity strategies: for identifying and rating critical functions; devising alternate, emergency methods; assessing their business impact; and performing cost-benefit analyses.

BUSINESS CONTINUITY STRATEGIES

Business continuity strategies are those actions that are implemented, once the emergency is under control, to restore the business to normalcy in the shortest possible time.

Such strategies include ways to process orders, handle customers and complaints and maintain cash flow until computer systems can be restored, or a building can be reoccupied.

In the end, continuity strategies represent options for the line managers who will decide which ones to employ given the particulars of any given situation.

Figure 4.6 on page 72 gives examples of what continuity strategies can look like. Many if not most of the strategies given here may also apply to your organization.

In Chapter 4 it was suggested that you begin this project by distributing copies of "Appendix A.2: Business Continuity Survey" on page 156 to others in the company at the start of the project. If you did and have gotten back the completed surveys, you're ahead of the game. If not, now is the time to do it because you will need the information for the next three exercises.

As an alternative you could devise a simpler survey by having each department simply respond to the following questions:

- If the on-line system used in your [name a critical function] was not available, how would you operate?

- What office equipment is used in this process, and could you operate for a period of three days without it? Seven days?

- What is the minimum office space and staff you would use to perform this process manually?

- What forms are needed, if any, to perform data entry?

- What communications equipment would be necessary to continue operations?

- What employees are cross-trained to perform other key functions?

When distributing surveys resist the temptation to omit seemingly unimportant units to cull the paperwork from the outset. Prejudging which departments do not perform critical tasks may result in serious holes in your plan when it is dusted off for execution in an actual crisis.

You will be in a better position during the planning process to determine which departments perform critical tasks and which ones play lesser roles only after you evaluate how each of the firm's departments view their contributions to the firm's mission, and how the various departments may actually be critically interdependent.

An example of this may be a large consulting firm that typically delivers its products via electronic transmissions. As a result, it may consider the mail room an unimportant anachronism. But during a crisis the firm may suddenly find itself in desperate need of packaging and delivering is products as physical documents. This point may be missed during the planning stage unless the mail room supervisor is included in the survey.

You may also want to "help" department managers complete surveys. You could couch your offer as a way for you to help them "save time."

Exercise 6: Compile survey responses into one list

However you choose to survey your organization, this exercise is to compile the critical functions responses as one list in the "Function" column of a blank Appendix A.6 on page 161. Ignore the *Criticality* (Cr.) and *Alternate Method* columns for now, and don't expect the list of functions to be in a final order as

Figure 6.1: Business continuity strategies example

Cr.	Function	Alternate Method
1	Administration	Transfer emergency grab kit to hot site upon activation. Set up emergency ops. Center (EOC) in activated site.
1	Administration, Job execution, Billing (A/R-P/R), Customer relations, Media liaison	Tap into host's power. If hot site is also out of normal power, use our emergency gas-powered generator 4 hours/day (with stored fuel for 40 hrs.) to charge up all equipment. Use laptop battery chargers hooked up to our alternate electrical power generator in the event of electrical outage.
1	Administration	Transfer 3 existing UPS devices in main office to hot site and hookup to emergency generator. Top off UPS during alt. power run. UPS to provide ongoing reserve power between alt. gen. runs.
2	Administration	Establish an EOC in hot site with table/chairs for ea. of 4 Dept. heads. Operate/manage all activities through normalization.
2	Administration	Employees to work from home; communicate via cell. phones if available, Co. Intranet if available, or daily courier runs between EOC and employees' homes.
2	Job execution	Use an alternate (wireless hotspot) Internet provider for research
2	Job scheduling	Use the latest available hard copy of the project deadlines.
3	Customer service	Refer to the latest hard copy of status of projects (PM program).
3	Customer service	Explain to customers that Internet/computer systems are down, but they will be informed of order status ASAP.
3	Job execution	Use the portable printer for project outputs if paper report is needed.
3	Job scheduling	Manually update/maintain the latest project schedules.
3	Order processing	Use latest copy of order status report to update work-in-progress.
3	Order processing	Record new project assignments manually.
3	Billing (A/R)	Prepare a short list of large billable amounts that need to be collected quickly and send out reminders and/or paper invoices.
3	Shipping	Generate a paper contact list for urgent shipping (where delay can influence/hurt our relationship with the customer).
3	Shipping	Notify customers about any possible delays in shipping.
4	Payroll	Store the most recent backup copy of payroll check images offsite.
4	Payroll	Issue checks manually and include a notice indicating that shortages or overages will be corrected at end of crisis.
4	Billing (A/P)	Defer payments less than $1,000 until computers and accounting records are restored.
4	Billing (A/R)	Invoice large dollar amounts (above $2,000) manually (paper estimates/proposals need to be available).

Cr. = criticality

shown in Figure 6.1. What's important now is to get a full list of perceived critical functions on one document. The remaining two columns will be completed in the next two exercises.

If you have a "plan creation team" or committee, the next two exercises present a good opportunity for the group to discuss together the interrelationships of the organization's critical functions, their relative importance to the organization's recovery, and how they can be performed manually.

"It's imperative that you suppress the impulse to rate too many functions as critical. The fewer the better. Too many critical tasks during a crisis will hamper your recovery."

The team's joint participation will reveal potential conflicts or oversights and will shorten the time needed for the various departments to agree and produce a final list of strategies.

Depending on the size of your organization, participants' buy-in could be important both in the formulation of the company's BCP and in its execution in a crisis. If your organization has departments do provide copies of a draft version of the anticipated continuity strategies worksheet to the department heads for final additions, changes, corrections or suggestions. This will give them ownership in the final product.

Exercise 7: Assess how critical functions impact your business

Use Table 6.1 to assign a criticality to each function on the list you created in Exercise 6 as you consider the following issues:

- Revenue stream
- Market value

- Retention of customers
- Operating costs
- Company's reputation
- A high profile client
- A legal or regulatory requirement

It's imperative that you suppress the impulse to rate too many functions as critical. The fewer the better. Too many critical tasks during a crisis will hamper your recovery. This bears repeating.

Critical functions will also have associated requirements that should be included in the BCP. For example, working payroll the "old fashioned" way, without an Internet connection or electricity, will require you at least have paper checks in the grab kit.

With that in mind, you may also want to show how each business function would operate during a stabilization period under two distinct scenarios: (a) when facilities are unusable and a

Table 6.1: Criticality ratings for business functions

Importance	Effect on the Organization
1 - Most Critical	Restore immediately to ensure the survival of the organization. Continued dysfunction would prevent other restoration efforts.
2 - Highly Critical	Disruption of this function exceeding 24 hours would jeopardize the business or raise it to a most critical status.
3 - Critical	Disruption of these exceeding three days would seriously impact the operation of the business.
4 - Secondary Impact	Disruption of these exceeding one to two weeks (depending on the business) would seriously impact operations.
5 - Non-critical Functions	Disruption of these would be an inconvenience, but would not seriously impact the operation of the business.

Source: Adapted from Butch Gelnovatch, 2003. "Business Continuity Planning" white paper.

dispersed workforce needs to work remotely, and (b) when facilities are usable.

Once you have assigned criticality scores you will know which ones on the list are truly critical, which ones are just important, and which ones are neither. Everything else the company does is, possibly, a distraction that you may consider discarding from the workload even in normal times.

Exercise 8: Develop manual ways to work critical functions

The final step in creating your business continuity strategies list is to identify or devise manual, alternate methods for performing each critical function *without grid power or the Internet.*

These are the functions you may, in a worst case crisis, have to perform remotely from an emergency location. All your tools need to be stand-alone and locally powered for an extended period of time, until normality is restored. How long depends on your risk assessment and your own judgement of what's reasonable. Major institutions and companies frequently plan to be self-sufficient for as long as two weeks.

At this point the list is still in draft form and the functions probably are not in order. If that's so, now is the time to produce a final, clean version of it in order of criticality and in a logical progression of work, as shown in Figure 6.1 on page 99.

This list can also have additional narrative pages that provide expanded information or more explicit instructions for executing some functions.

COST-BENEFIT ANALYSIS

There may be times when the cost of a function's alternative methods are not clear and you may need to compare your options. One of the best tools available for that is what is known as the cost-benefit analysis, or CBA.

Another objective of a CBA is to look beyond the obvious gains and losses to consider factors that are indirectly related to the issue but can have significant and unintended consequences rather than the expected outcome. Such unrelated factors may

Figure 6.2: Cost-benefit analysis example

ALTERNATE SITE COSTS AND BENEFITS/YEAR				
LINE ITEM	PRESENT ARRANGE.	COLD SITE	WARM SITE	HOT SITE
Rotation backups	400	400	400	400
Online backups	1,200	1,200	1,200	N/A
Room availability contract	N/A	750	N/A	N/A
Room rent (600/sf)[1]	2,100	1,000	13,400	13,400
ADP equipment/files[2]	600	600	1,000	1,000
Telephone lines (2)	500	400	3,000	3,000
Facsimile line[3]	400	400	3,000	3,000
Portable office kit	300	300	300	300
Yearly test[4]	1,000	1,000	850	750
BOP insurance	3,000	3,000	2,200	1,500
SUBTOTALS	**9,500**	**9,050**	**25,350**	**25,350**
Risk Factor[5]	1.4	1.2	1.1	1.0
Potential operational cost	**13,300**	**10,860**	**27,885**	**23,350**
Recovery time	5 days	3 days	2 days	4 hours
Revenue loss/nonoperational day	4,000	4,000	4,000	4,000
Potential lost revenues	20,000	12,000	8,000	670
TOTAL COSTS[6]	**33,300**	**22,860**	**35,885**	**24,020**
Cost-Benefit Ranking	3	1	4	2

1 Cost for a two-week emergency period, or for interrupted business testing. Warm and hot site options assume continuous room occupancy and availability year-round.
2 ADP equipment costs are amortized over five years.
3 This older technology may be replaced by a similarly priced secure system.
4 Yearly interrupted business testing that requires one or more days as necessary to assure system integrity and function.
5 Subjective risk factor of cost miscalculations due to scarcity in a widespread crisis or difficulties from inadequate preparations.
6 Considers maintenance and projected costs during an actual crisis or business interruption test in a given year.

be unexpected or unacceptable time usage/waste or lowered employee morale.

Yet another benefit of a CBA is that it synthesizes the financial impacts an incident could cause into rough (or accurate) comparisons between competing outcomes to a threat response.

Assessing impact is central to conducting a CBA. It can be a reasonably simple task or highly complex.

There seems to be no standard way to perform any sort of cost-benefit-analysis, although they are approached in one of two basic ways: (a) using at least several basic real-world figures regarding the activity's costs for achieving a certain result, such as a critical business function, to serve as reference points; and (b) extrapolating values from theoretical models.

Of these two, the first one is useful for our purposes. But to compare alternatives, the reference points used for each comparison must be the same.

The usual and best common denominator for a CBA analysis is money (but not always). Thus, each option's cost and desirability is reduced to a dollar value (or other unit) for direct comparisons.

An estimate is used when a factor does not easily reduce to an exact value. Figure 6.2 illustrates a CBA calculation for choosing an alternate site.

CBAs usually follow one more rule: offer at least three comparable choices whenever possible, one of which is always "do nothing differently" vis-à-vis other distinct alternatives.

For crisis preparation purposes, the important point of a cost-benefit analysis is to have a recovery plan and know its time and monetary costs.

An exercise is not included for preparing a CBA because they aren't normally a BCP component; they are only a decision-making tool, and they can vary so much regarding the number of comparable options and the factors to use. However, a generic, modifiable CBA template that's similar to this example is available as a spreadsheet for download from quest-publishing.com/resources.

Figure 6.3: Emergency contact list example

EMERGENCY CONTACT LIST

Building Crisis Center	Hartman Bldg., Suite 711
Building Manager's Name/Telephone	Manuel Hernandez/305-445-8778
Fire/Rescue Services	911 (non-emergency: 305-460-5582
Miami-Dade Office of Emergency Mgt.	305-468-5400
Local Police Departments	
City of Miami	305-442-5555 (James Haley, Chief)
County Sheriff's Office	305-468-5400 (Mike Johnson, Sheriff)
Bomb Disposal	911
Hazardous Materials/Telephone	Miami-Dade Co. Haz. Mgt. Bureau / 911
Electric Company	FPL
Contact	Joan Fontain (for Hartman Bldg.)
In Case of Outage	Manuel Hernandez/786-441-4445
Water Company	Miami-Dade Water & Sewer/305-445-7777
In Case of Outage	John Adams/305-665-3545
Telephone Company	BellSouth/866-620-6000
Contact	Adam Campos (for Hartman Bldg.)
In Case of Outage	305-665-3765
Internet Provider	Allgood Communications
Contact	Paul Allgood/305-777-4560
Ordering, Billing, Other Services	866-620-6000
Medical Facilities	Baptist Hospital (3.7 miles)
Address	5000 University Drive, Miami, FL 33224
Telephone	911 (non-emergency: 305-666-2111)
Alternate Relocation Site	Regus (Suite 722 in CitiPlace Bldg.)
Warm Site	2404 14th Street, Doral, FL 34356
Telephone	305-345-8787
Business Insurance Company	BizMit Insurance Co.
Point of Contact	Ben Stratton, Account Exec.
Address	1004 Main Street, Boston, MA 88765
Telephone	800-676-4761
Media Contact	Miami Business Chronicle
Point of Contact	Linda Harper, Int'l Business Editor
Address	4321 Federal Street, Miami, FL 33135
Telephone	305-441-8877 X4455

EMERGENCY CONTACTS

Among the most useful tools to have in a fast-breaking crisis is the ability to sound the alarm and summon help. Once the crisis is manageable there will be many people and organizations to communicate with, from responders and employees to suppliers and clients. A final task for the crisis management section of your BCP is to produce a thorough contact list.

Exercise 9: Build your emergency contacts list

Use a blank emergency contacts worksheet (Appendix A.7 on page 162) to build the list of contacts that are external to your organization, from first responders and media to suppliers and vendors, and facilities like hospitals and shelters you may need to make use of during a crisis. What goes into this list depends on your region, your needs and the resources you can line up before a crisis. Figure 6.3 is an example of such a list.

■ ■ ■

Given the range of things that can go wrong, a business can suffer a crisis at any time, from its early, formative months, to well into a long successful run.

When a crisis happens—whether it affects only some systems or is a major catastrophy that takes everything down at once— you will be thankful that you planned to continue your business.

You will be able to avert most crises through an early warning system. Even if the business suffers losses to people, property or market share from a crisis you cannot avoid your business is likely survive if you managed the risks and took the precautionary steps to mitigate the worst possible outcome.

Good planning is the key to effective crisis management.

7

ARRESTING THE FALL

We are what we repeatedly do. Excellence,
therefore, is not an act but a habit.

— Aristotle

SKYDIVERS PRACTICE THEIR skill under severe time frames. Time is not on their side; critical events unfold fast. An ill-conceived emergency response or no action can quickly prove fatal.

Knowing this, they study efficient emergency procedures for each possible "malfunction" they may encounter. Then they practice, practice, practice … until their responses to a range of potential failures are reflexive and appropriate. In an emergency, they have only seconds to save their lives! "Your plan is your parachute" is more than a metaphor for them.

Time in a company crisis can also be critical, possibly measured in seconds or minutes, as in the case of a structural failure or a rapidly spreading fire.

Other crises, though, will give more time to react appropriately: hours if not days. Whether the crisis is "exploding" or manifesting less quickly, there's a protocol to follow that's described in the Risk Intelligence and Solutions Cycle (illustrated on page 38). In this chapter we'll focus on steps 2 to 5 of the cycle, which can be summarized in the following three points:

- respond appropriately to a breaking crisis to safeguard the lives and well-being of everyone in the organization's purview; and then,

- secure facilities and assets as a secondary consideration; followed by,

- media relations and containment of the crisis to mitigate the event's harm.

Everything else in the BCP will wait until you have managed these three tasks. So now let's discuss some important considerations during the breaking part of a crisis.

GOOD CRISIS RESPONSE HABITS

Armed robberies pose an example of a rapidly unfolding crisis that is realistic for many businesses, particularly convenience stores, jewelry stores and banks—or any valuables or cash business open to the public.

"Whatever the crisis, it's human nature to
fall back on habits when under stress."

Protecting employees and customers should be foremost in their minds. Similarly, workplace violence by a deranged or emotional employee or patron can unfold very quickly in any business.

A well thought-out response must be planned before it happens in order to save lives or the very business. Once strategies are formulated, personnel must be equipped and practiced.

Whatever the crisis, it's human nature to fall back on *habits* when under stress. The Plan Administrator's challenge is to create the right organizational reflexes to fall back on when responding to a crisis.

DECLARING AND ENDING A CRISIS

If your business doesn't send out a clear alarm for a breaking crisis, how will those responsible know to kick into high gear? What if it isn't fast-breaking? At what point should the alarm be tripped? Who sounds the alarm?

Triggering a crisis response should be the responsibility of a clearly identified individual or a company position. The BCP should include a section where responsible individuals (by names or positions) are charged with declaring the start of a crisis and under what circumstances to initiate one. It can also be a tripwire, like an alarm.

Some organizations appoint different positions to trigger different types of crises. For instance, the chief information officer (CIO) may be designated to invoke an information systems crisis while the building manager may declare a facility emergency. In more cases, though, one person, the site manager or principal officer, reserves the duty for herself, guided by her executives.

If warning signals are not detected early enough then a crisis is likely to manifest itself rapidly; thus, there must be someone capacitated at all times to sound the alarm and send response teams into action. It will do no good if the one person with authority is inaccessible when the crisis breaks and those who

Figure 7.1: Crisis response actions worksheet example

Responsibility	Action
Manager on duty	Notify proper authorities (police, fire, utility departments, etc.)
Production Shop Warden	Maintain signage and lead evacuations from production shop area
Front Office Warden	Maintain signage and lead evacuations from front office/sales
CMT (ERT)	Determine if the disaster recovery/bus. cont. plan is activated
CMT (ERT)	Notify employees of emergency (if declared)
CMT (ERT)	Arrange transportation to alternative site
CMT (ERT)	Instruct dept. managers to implement bus. cont. strategies
CMT (ERT)	Notify senior management
CEO/Principal	Distribute a pre-drafted or original press release if appropriate
COO	Manage staging site setup and operation
Legal	Notify insurance carrier
Admin. Manager	Notify alternative (cold) site vendor of need
Admin. Manager	Arrange for transport/setup of supplies to alternative site
Research Director	Implement paper-based research strategies
Research Director	Inform clients of changed deliverables dates (if so)
Finances Director	Implement paper-based job control and accounting system
Reconstruction Team	Assess damage
Reconstruction Team	Arrange for facility cleanup and reconstruction
Reconstruction Team	Salvage usable equipment
Tech. Outsource Team	Bring up backup data and reconfigure computer systems
Tech. Outsource Team	Test computers and equipment
Admin. Manager	Reintegrate employees to primary facility
Legal	File insurance claims

could act to mitigate it cannot. This function should always rest with someone on call or on duty.

The fewer the employees a company has the easier it is to identify who can initiate a response. Larger organizations need a clear chain of command, but with a group dedicated to the task of crisis management and recovery: the crisis management team (CMT), a practiced group of company specialists working as a microcosm of the larger company.

Just as someone needs to be charged with response initiation, so must someone be charged with declaring it over or people will continue in crisis mode longer than necessary.

Exercise 10: Create a crisis response program

This step is to identify the actions to be taken and the people assigned the responsibility for taking them as soon as a crisis happens. Figure 7.1 illustrates the result of this exercise for our All Colors Printing Company case study.

As you read through the following sections consider what is relevant to your organization and enter your responses into a blank crisis response program worksheet (Appendix A.8 on page 164).

A logical place to start this worksheet is with this entry: identify the individual or company position normally responsible for *triggering* the organization into crisis mode. Follow that with the list of individuals or positions that are to continue to take the actions necessary to front and control the crisis.

EVACUATIONS

Different crises, like a fire, earthquake or a bomb threat, may require different responses. A common thread to all crises is to vacate a physical facility as quickly as possible—but without panic, which can lead to a dangerous stampede or failure to find good exits. The antidote to panic is control, familiarity and signage.

Just as someone needs to be charged with response initiation, so must someone be charged with declaring it over or people will continue in crisis mode longer than necessary.

Control is achieved through "ward" assignments. That means that your plan will list by name or position what persons are named "wardens" and are charged with keeping exits functioning within their sector; that is, their assigned area, section or wing.

A sector's warden and its occupants are responsible for knowing and following crisis response procedures and physically moving themselves and their visitors to safety when an evacuation is triggered.

The number of wardens that a facility should have depends on its size, architecture, and the number of exits, stairways and floors.

Familiarity is achieved through the practice of emergency procedures on a scheduled basis. Keep attrition and turnover in mind.

Signage, the posting of evacuation floor maps and clear markings of pathways to exit points, is what people can respond to successfully in pandemonium, or if visibility is reduced.

Signage can be audible signals, like a continuous beep, emitted from an exit point to draw evacuees to it. A sound system can guide evacuees from one point to another up to an exit even blinded. But to be useful in a crises electrical emergency devices should be driven by uninterrupted power supply (UPS) sources.

Most threats will likely require a quick evacuation from a facility but some, like the threat of an active shooter or an armed robbery, can require an opposite reaction: a lockdown or a shelter-in-place. Planning, practice and wardens make the difference between mitigation and an unmitigated disaster.

At the very least, your BCP plan should include evacuation diagrams and warden assignments.

Figure 7.2: Crisis grab kit worksheet example

Qty.	Item Description	Team/Purpose	Destination
2	Walkie-talkie radios	Communications	Staging 1
2	Battery powered emergency lights	Operations	Staging 1
1	10'x20' pop-up canopy tent with sides	Operations	Staging 1
2	Walkie-talkie radios	Communications	Staging 2
2	Battery powered emergency lights	Communications	Staging 2
1	10'x10' pop-up canopy tent with sides	Operations	Staging 2
1	Company policies and procedures manual	Administration	Warm site
1	Printout of customers list and contact info	Communications	Warm site
1	Radio base station with repeater	Communications	Warm site
2	Spare/backup radios + charging station	Communications	Warm site
1	Company IT database backup disk	Data Restoration	Warm site
1	Insurance policies binder	Legal	Warm site
1	Office tools set (stapler, hole punch, etc.)	Operations	Warm site
2	Notebook PC	Operations	Warm site
1	Laser printer with 4 sets replace cartridges	Operations	Warm site
1	Portable power generation plant	Operations	Warm site
50	Gallons of fuel	Operations	Warm site
2	Battery-powered emergency lights	Operations	Warm site
100	C-cell batteries for resupply	Operations	Warm site
...	...	...	...

CRISIS RESPONSE GRAB KIT

An effective response to a breaking crisis is possible with the availability of the right tools, supplies, equipment and information to continue functioning in the absence of your normal environment.

So far we've disdussed the many things and actions you need to be ready for a crisis, and who in your organization is responsible for them. Now you need to list the many things you may want to include in your mobile physical emergency kit—a crisis "grab kit" that amounts to the "parachute" that will arrest your fall and soften your landing.

Exercise 11: Produce your emergency/crisis grab kit list

Having given thought and having conferred with your organization's crisis team members about what items should be listed in the crisis grab kit, produce a written list.

Your perception of a worst-case crisis and your organization's needs to meet such an event can be very different from other businesses even in the same industry, but consider the following things as you create a grab kit for your particular needs:

- Communications (radios, cell. and satellite phones, etc.)
- Company electronic database (backup disk or device)
- Physical copies of important documents and books
- Portable emergency generator and fuel
- Portable lighting (like flashlights, extra batteries)
- Portable computers and calculators
- Mobile furniture (folding tables, chairs, etc.)
- Common office tools
- Sheltering (tarps, tents, sleeping bags, etc.)
- Survival tools (like multi-use knives, etc.)
- Tool kit (for provisional construction, installation, repairs)
- First aid kit and medications for your special needs
- Emergency rations
- Water purification system
- Clothing (for work and survival)

Once you have created the list have the crisis response team members review it. Assure it's complete. Then procure and store the items away from the normal facility. You will likely adjust the kit when your team "exercises" and sees the need for other gear to include in the grab kit.

PAPER VERSION OF YOUR BCP

Some crises will deny your business of every form of normal

resources, like energy, telephone service (wire or cellular), and access to the Internet. So, you'll want to be sure you have in your grab kit at least one copy of the full business continuity plan so critical information is always available to your recovery team.

In fact, more than one copy is advisable for your grab kit if your plan scatters people to different locations other than the principal alternate facility. Keep enough copies in the grab kit to supply each location with one along with supplies they need.

THE MEDIA IN A BREAKING CRISIS

A media presence is not likely to be an issue for most organizations during a natural disaster or a data loss (unless it's a major breach), but media relations are extremely important for a range of crisis that deal with the comportment or image of the company. Immediate steps should be taken to blunt negative media coverage when the crisis involves responsibility issues, such as contaminants, accidents, labor matters or personnel incidents. Those types of crisis can damage the business needlessly if the media is shirked off or if the company appears to withhold information.

Once the crisis is known to be one of image or responsibility, company executives should immediately issue an appropriate press release. A press release can be quick and well-conceived by basing it on one of the press releases pre-written during the planning phase.

Image damage control will be far easier if the company followed a "media relations program" prior to the crisis. Established contacts with friendly reporters do not guarantee the kind of coverage you would like to see, but reporters who perceive openness and cooperation from a friendly face are more likely to give the benefit of the doubt.

Once an image or responsibility type of crisis breaks, or is about to, do not hesitate to deal with the media if you are

approached. Avoiding them only invites greater, possibly negative, interest.

■   ■   ■

The best crisis management outcomes result from activities to
avoid them in the first place. And properly equipped you'll be
able to successfully negotiate the crises that you do have to face.

This chapter walked you through the tools and actions your
organization should have ready to deploy as soon as an early
warning signal goes off. In the worst of cases you may only have
seconds, or minutes, to deploy your parachute.

8

LANDING A CRISIS

The pessimist complains about the wind;
the optimist expects it to change;
the realist adjusts the sails.

— William Arthur Ward

A N OLD JOKE you may have heard before goes like this: "It's not the fall that kills you—it's the sudden stop!" We can all agree on that. So in this chapter we discuss what needs to be done to ride your business down from a breaking crisis in free fall to a soft landing under a business continuity parachute.

Our focus here is on steps 6 (diagnosis) and 7 (recovery) of the Risk Intelligence and Solutions Cycle on page 38. This includes the activities and strategies an organization needs to recover losses, restore customer and vendor relations, and resume operations from work intake to product deliveries and the critical internal services that make operations possible.

WHAT HAPPENED?

Once a fire has started and everyone is busy putting it out it doesn't help to know that a smoke alarm failed to sound; but it is very important, for example, to know (and act on) that a company employee has been struggling with depression and work performance and just stormed off in a threatening huff after being fired.

You can start your research while you deploy continuity strategies but the deep analysis of the cause will come after the crisis is over and you look for lessons learned in step 8 of the RISC map.

The purpose of introspection during the landing phase should be to avoid further harm by aftershocks while you manage an active crisis.

ALTERNATE COMMUNICATIONS

An emergency call up and business continuity depends on communications. Once you know where responders and suppliers could be you can think about ways to reach them in case cables and cellular repeaters are down, if Internet service is interrupted, or if the roads are impassable.

Technology has made our lives more convenient. Today we can be in touch 24 hours a day, almost anywhere, but you may have to revert to older technology. Figure 8.1 shows a variety of communications methods you can consider employing to communicate between public emergency services, your own crisis center and crisis responders, employees, customers, suppliers or the media during emergencies.

ALTERNATE INFORMATION AND DATA

The continuity of your organization's business is the job of its owners. Public emergency response services, like police or fire

Figure 8.1: Emergency methods of communication

- Hand signals (within line of sight)
- Messengers (beyond line of sight)
- Two-way radios (limited range)
- Facsimile machines
- Ham radio (long-range)
- Hardwired telephones
- Cellular/radio telephones
- Local area networks and intranets
- Satellite telephones
- Internet (comm. apps, twitter, email, etc.)
- Satellite links

departments, are tasked with protecting life, health and property—not corporate entities *per se*.

How long you need to be self-sufficient depends on your industry and your organization. You shouldn't count on public services during a regional crisis when they'll be preoccupied executing their own continuity plan for everyone in their jurisdiction.

After you've reestablished communications, or if you didn't lose it, your next move toward a soft landing is to regain the company's data.

It's up to your business to provide the resources you need to survive the landing to operating normalcy.

Emergency Equipment

An organization's lifeblood, its records, depends on a number of actions you can take to prevent or overcome the loss of data. Foremost among those actions are the availability and maintenance of certain emergency equipment discussed below:

Alternate power source in case electricity is lost. Major disasters typically affect wide geographic areas and can take days or weeks to restore power. (In the very worst of cases you could be without electricity or potable water for months.) Prudent organizations plan for this event and maintain one or more emergency generators and the requisite fresh fuel to last at least two weeks.

Uninterrupted power supply (UPS) devices for computers are handy for major or minor power interruptions, which typically occur at inopportune moments. Without a UPS, a power loss of any duration, even a fraction of a second, will erase a computer's volatile memory. These events can cause the loss of hours of work that has not been saved, and the disruption can also lead to corruption. Most UPS devices also serve as surge protectors.

Alternate dial-up lines and modems to replace primary Internet or Intranet connections. These will earn their keep as long as telephone lines are intact. Their slow transmission speeds will be tolerable when there are no other means to send and receive facsimiles or access electronic mail and web sites.

Anti-virus software protects against cyber attacks. These programs guard against a host of malicious scripts that are self-propagating and programmed to penetrate operating system weaknesses to interrupt or destroy electronic files.

A recent form of attack is "ransomware" in which the criminal who succeeds in accessing your computer installs malware that encrypts the entire disk and locks the computer up and demands a ransom payment in cryptocurrency for the "key" (code) to undo the damage, which you may or may not get. The best defense against this is to have a reliable backup system that can be used to recover or replace the affected device or devices.

On-site insulated vaults are used to store one duplicate set of your most critical records in both electronic and paper format:

- Tape or disk back-ups for full restorations
- Employee, vendor and customer accounts information
- Warranties and services agreements
- Financial and insurance information
- Intellectual property and trade secrets
- Technical plans and drawings
- Personnel files

Data Backup Strategies

Your most important protective measure will be a disciplined electronic data backup routine that includes periodic full backups rather than incremental backups. The frequency of backups depends on your risk tolerance and type of business.

Periodic backup rotations are reasonable backup strategies but require discipline. In this case, companies backup automatically on a daily basis but rotate external tapes or drives weekly. Upon rotation, the tape or disk is transferred to an alternate site sufficiently distanced from the primary site so the same regional crisis is unlikely to affect both.

Upon transfer, the backup is immediately tested (restored) using the alternate site's backup computers to assure its integrity and to practice your "recovery team" in the process.

If a backup is discovered to be flawed then, it can be replaced immediately. The backup at the alternate site is then transferred to the primary site's insulated vault.

In all, this strategy has three backups at one time: copy A in the primary site's computer, copy B in the alternate site, and copy C in the primary site's vault.

This strategy can be simplified by performing fewer backups or storing them in fewer places. For example, you can maintain just one backup (in the primary machine in the event the hard disk corrupts) and one in the alternate location.

Mirrored computers are yet another way for a very small business to assure the integrity of its data. With this method the company simply duplicates the hard drive of its main system onto another desktop or a portable (notebook) computer. Available commercial software will literally "mirror" the contents of one hard drive onto another so it is an exact replica of the first.

Mirroring software for synchronizing files between your main computer and other computers in your intranet is still used. The trend now is to mirror a physical device (notebook, desktop or server) in your control to a "managed data warehouse in the cloud." That's a good thing as long as you have a working Internet connection.

Online backup services (cloud-based services) are simpler and give the assurance that backed up data is safely stored away in a remote location. The simplicity encourages frequent full backups.

When using an online data service for backups be sure to set it to backup files one-way up to the online service. The down path should be to a separate local storage device.

Some services are dedicated strictly to cloud backups of your business or personal devices and not for online storage. This is a good alternative if your goal for cloud service is only to backup. If you need online storage as well you'll want to read on.

Cloud services like Microsoft's OneDrive, GoogleDrive, Amazon AWS and Apple iCloud are the behemoths of the industry and do more than just backup: they can provide online storage to extend the disk space on local devices, or mirror the disk on a local computer, plus a host of other business services.

In addition to these four, there are hundreds of smaller companies providing online backup and storage services. Many of these are built on the platforms of Google, Amazon or Microsoft and inherit the safety and features of these.

These services offer continuous synchronizing with a localized server or a desktop. That means that if files disappear from your computer the deletions will replicate in the online copy unless you catch the deletion quickly enough to stop the system from synchronizing.

The saving grace to such an error is that the online services backup their systems continuously and can restore (roll back) your online database to an earlier date and time, before a deletion or corruption occurred.

Once you restore the online copy you can complete your recovery of deleted files or clean a corrupted directory by mirroring the online instance to your local device.

Be mindful, though, that most online backup/storage providers offer free basic accounts. Features to restore an online database are usually reserved for fee-based accounts. So, if your goal is to backup files, and not just use the service for free storage, you'll probably need to upgrade to a paid service.

External hard drives can be attached directly to a server or desktop computer. That makes these an even simpler way to back up critical data.

In an emergency, the hard drive containing a duplicate of the company data could simply be disconnected from the main system and transported to the alternate site to be hooked up to another computer and resume data usage.

Of these strategies, an online backup service illustrated in Figure 8.2 may be the most convenient for a small business. But take the extra step to backup the online service to a local, physical hard drive periodically as well, if you can. It's added insurance.

If you do that, the extra backup drive could feed from a mirrored computer kept at your warm or hot site (if you have one) or at a satellite office, but not in the same place where the main system resides.

In case you need to, you can restore your devices from a cloud rollback, or you can copy the external hard drive's data to a computer, or duplicate the external drive and access data from the copy.

ALTERNATE FACILITIES

An alternate site is where you will conduct your business in the event your normal, primary facility becomes inoperable. Arrangements for them can be costly and time consuming but are essential to keeping a business alive in a crisis.

Assembly Areas and Accountability

Your crisis response plan should specify at least one assembly point in the event the primary site becomes unusable due to a natural disaster, fire, contamination, explosion or other hazard.

Consider that an evacuation can occur during off-hours and your critical and secondary personnel could be widely dispersed from the primary site when the crisis breaks.

An assembly point should not be another nearby building that may also become inoperable; it should be an open-air place, like a shaded parking lot. Additionally, there should be a second assembly point as well in a different part of the area in the event the first one is not accessible to all.

When designating open-air sites consider that you'll probably need quick setup sheltering for your crisis grab kit to protect your people and equipment from the elements in case the evacuation is prolonged.

As you plan consider distancing the separate sites so you can deploy a rudimentary communications system (messengers and/ or two-way radios) between the primary site, the alternate site, and the assembly points.

Your plan may create a "communications team" to maintain and operate a network of two-way or ham radios. The size

Figure 8.2: Simple emergency/crisis response infrastructure

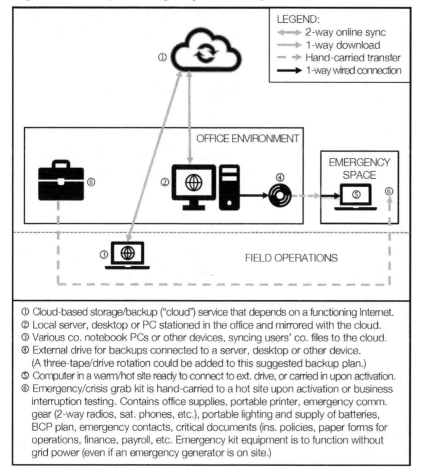

① Cloud-based storage/backup ("cloud") service that depends on a functioning Internet.
② Local server, desktop or PC stationed in the office and mirrored with the cloud.
③ Various co. notebook PCs or other devices, syncing users' co. files to the cloud.
④ External drive for backups connected to a server, desktop or other device.
  (A three-tape/drive rotation could be added to this suggested backup plan.)
⑤ Computer in a warm/hot site ready to connect to ext. drive, or carried in upon activation.
⑥ Emergency/crisis grab kit is hand-carried to a hot site upon activation or business
  interruption testing. Contains office supplies, portable printer, emergency comm.
  gear (2-way radios, sat. phones, etc.), portable lighting and supply of batteries,
  BCP plan, emergency contacts, critical documents (ins. policies, paper forms for
  operations, finance, payroll, etc. Emergency kit equipment is to function without
  grid power (even if an emergency generator is on site.)

and function of your organization will dictate to what length you should prepare; but when all other communications fail in a wide area, ham radios (or satellite telephones) may be the only way to reach the "outside world."

Once assembled, take a roll call and assure everyone's safety. Unaccounted-for persons must be traced by determining when they were last seen and where. In most cases that information should be passed to public emergency responders for action rather than initiate your own search-and-rescue efforts that may only worsen a bad situation.

Your organization's task is to organize your people, get them assembled and accounted for, and maintain the best level of communications possible between the pockets of people.

Sites to Suit the Budget and Risk Tolerance

Alternate business sites come in three flavors, each offering its own advantages and disadvantages, but it usually boils down to cost, as exemplified in "Figure 6.2: Cost-benefit analysis example" on page 103:

Hot sites contain all the same equipment as its corresponding primary sites, albeit down-sized for a smaller group, and are capable of resuming full operations within an hour.

Warm sites differ from hot sites in that they contain only the necessary hardware, and restoration will take longer because they must still be configured from backups. Also, the lack of all the equipment, essential as well as non-essential, will cause some inconveniences and delays throughout the crisis.

Cold sites are simply empty, electrified office spaces that are ready to accept the essential machines and files to resume operations.

They take far longer to get up and running because everything has to be set up from the beginning. When relying on a cold site make sure the needed equipment and files will be available and transportable to the site.

Do not rely on transferring your emergency grab kit from the primary site because a crisis could render it inaccessible. The full grab kit should be stored away from the primary site it's intended to supplant. Depending on the size of your grab kit and your organization's arrangements, it could be stored at a self-storage rental unit, a company officer's private home, a satellite office or branch, or in the alternate hot, warm or cold site itself.

Which of these three alternatives you choose to establish will depend on your organization's size and budget. Larger businesses will probably count on a hot or warm site, whereas small businesses may consider a simple contractual agreement for a cold site.

The midst of a crisis is no time to be looking for alternate space or recovery resources. You will be engrossed with managing the problem and you will probably have to make do with the resources you anticipated needing and arranged for. This is especially true for a community-wide or regional crisis.

Agreements

Contractual agreements for a standby cold site are indispensable if you want to be assured that a vendor will place your needs ahead of others during a widespread crisis. Such a contract will cost a fee but it will ensure the availability of space.

Another advantage of a contract is that you should be able to lock in the "occupancy" rate before demand drives up rates. The contract will assure your priority and price.

"Do not rely on transferring your emergency grab kit from the primary site because a crisis could render it inaccessible. The full grab kit should be stored away from the primary site it's intended to supplant."

Reciprocal agreements are another way of assuring the availability of an alternate site. In this arrangement two or more companies agree (in writing) to provide the other with an alternate site (hot, warm or cold) in the event of a crisis or a test. The partners should be distanced so the same widespread crisis is unlikely to affect the other.

Such agreements are beneficial because they are cost-effective for both since each other's primary sites will already be set up with telephone and Internet access and will have power. If you can agree to maintain warm sites at each other's locations your business will hardly miss a beat, but a cold site is also practical.

In either case, the only thing you or your partner need to do is give up one room temporarily and to run telephone extensions into the room until the other one recovers. Your task will be to furnish it with the essential systems and restore the backup.

Small businesses will be able to operate with one or two notebook computers.

PHYSICAL SECURITY CONSIDERATIONS

Emergencies have a way of causing extraordinary physical security problems. You will be more efficient and act more quickly if you are prepared beforehand with the necessary equipment for foreseen contingencies.

If your company deals with potential contaminants, for instance, you should have decontamination equipment and strategies on hand. You will not be able to collect equipment fast enough to respond to the crisis once it starts. And if you store a lot of valuables you need to be ready to safeguard them when responders, media and other "strangers" start to wander around.

RECOVERY AND RESTORATION

A recovery team is essential to restoration. The composition of such teams should have been determined during the planning phase and may vary according to the type of crisis. In the case of a data loss, the recovery team will be different from a communications loss recovery team, or the group that would handle a hazardous materials incident. And incidents that deal with company responsibility will likely be staffed with legal, personnel and operations executives. The following functions may require different teams:

- Damage assessment
- Physical security (to secure facilities and equipment)
- Alternate site storage and equipment
- Human resources (if the organization is sizable)
- Legal and insurance (to handle claims)
- Media relations

A better alternative for small businesses is to organize just one team with cross-trained members. The one team would then cover each of the foregoing functions as necessary with the one functional representative as "team leader" for the activity he or she is specialized in.

Salvage and Inventory Property

Once damage is assessed and security is established, your next move in the recovery process will be to salvage what you can. Using the inventory list prepared during the planning phase, begin the process of replacing what was lost through insurance claims or outright purchases of essential equipment that was not insured and you must replace anyway.

Resume Operations

In the final steps of recovery, you will put equipment back into working order and restore data if it has not already been done.

Then contact customers and vendors to resume operations using the continuity strategies in your plan.

Unless you have performed several business disruption tests before the crisis and discovered your plan's flaws beforehand, you will invariably find that the strategies will need some adaptations.

■   ■   ■

The ability to stay in business—to continue operating—even when denied facilities, people, assets or normal processes will depend on how well you steeled the organization. The crisis that throws you into turmoil may be relatively small and short, or it may be catastrophic and of long duration (weeks or months). Your business can recover from those with planning and preparation.

What isn't covered at all in this book are cataclysms—events of such magnitude that they literally change the course of history and humanity.

Less severe and more relatable are catastrophes like the 2004 Indian Ocean tsunami that killed over 230,000 and destroyed swaths of coastal communities throughout the Pacific basin and beyond, the 2011 9.0 earthquake in Japan, and the recent California wildfires. Such events could affect almost any organization almost anywhere. There are hardly any communities that aren't exposed to some natural hazard or human-caused calamity. The right plan and crisis grab kit will be indispensable for simple human survival in most any event.

PART

READY YOUR PARACHUTE

In this section you'll find the chapters that guide you through the final assembly—stitching the exercise worksheets that comprise the parts of your parachute into an actionable emergency document—and testing the final product on a continuing basis to be sure the initial plan works, and then to keep it current.

C H A P T E R

9

SEW UP YOUR PARACHUTE

*Say all you have to say in the fewest possible
words, or your reader will be sure to skip
them; and in the plainest possible words or
he will certainly misunderstand them.*

— John Ruskin

IN AN ORGANIZATION the institutional memory is recorded
in writing as policies and procedures, and through team practice
and their after action reports.

A written plan is essential to preserve the findings of your
preparations and research and to organize myriad tasks that will
need to be executed *reflexively* under a time crunch. What has not
been thought out and reduced to a crisis response plan prior to a
crisis will very likely be ill conceived or foregone.

This chapter will help you gather your responses to exercises
in previous chapters and record your plan as a succinct written
document.

PLAN OBJECTIVES

As you write the BCP keep the four emergency management objectives in mind:

Prevention, that is, maintaining the security of physical structures and data, and the like. This strives to institutionalize whatever steps should be taken to avert the likelihood of a disaster, including minimizing the impact if one does occur.

Recovery of essential business functions. Document how the organization will continue despite a disaster.

Accountability during normal operations, emergency response, and stabilization periods. Assign responsibilities to specific individuals and hold them accountable.

Compliance audits that institutionalize business continuity plans, including regular testing as part of the program, and "learn" from these activities to keep the BCP fresh.

WAYS TO PRESENT YOUR PLAN

If you have completed the worksheets offered in the preceding chapters you are ready to assemble your parachute—a polished business continuity plan for your organization.

A BCP report template is not provided in this book, but the bulk of the work is already done. You have two options for presenting your information: a running narrative or a short, cover policy memo with worksheets as appendices to the BCP.

Figure 9.1 is an example of what a brief BCP policy memo can look like. Note that it serves as a cover for appended worksheets that can be easily updated without redoing an entire report. The following sections show two ways to present the plan.

Figure 9.1: Simplified business continuity plan

MEMORANDUM

Date: June 10
To: CEO, ABC Inc.
From: Chief Operations Officer
Subject: Business Continuity Plan

EXECUTIVE SUMMARY

This contingency plan is primarily designed to protect against the sudden loss of telephone service, computer processing capability, or access to vital facilities. A disaster might be caused by an incident such as accidental fire, arson, contamination by hazardous material, aircraft accident, tornado, windstorm, or earthquake. Experience indicates the probability of such a disaster occurring at given installation is remote. However, owing to present and planned dependency on technology and vital facilities, "what if" business continuity strategies have been developed to protect our people and the critical business functions that will allow us to continue to operate and service our customers until normal processing capability is restored.

It is expected that computer operations will be restored within one or two weeks. In a worst case scenario these business continuity strategies could be in effect longer. Although temporary discontinuance of some systems may result in a loss of efficiency, the objective is to prevent a significant deterioration in cash and/or the ability to service customers during a stabilization period.

POLICY

The contingency plan policy of ABC Inc. is to (1) ensure an organized and effective response to an isolated disaster that would render telephone communications, remote data communication, and/or computer equipment inaccessible or inoperative, or normal work locations inaccessible, and (2) ensure business continuity for business functions dependent on computer technology until normal processing capability is restored....

SCOPE

It is the goal of ABC Inc. to be fully productive during normal business hours. Any incident that prevents us from doing so will be addressed and corrected in accordance with this Business Continuity Plan. Since each disaster is unique, this plan will not attempt to address specific disaster scenarios and the detailed steps involved in recovering from them. Rather, the purpose of this document is to provide corrective measures applicable to any situation by preparing for the worst-case scenario. As such, this document contains information concerning our assets and inventory, the names

Simplified business continuity plan (continued)

and numbers of business contacts, vendors, customers, insurance companies, and civil authorities whom we may need to contact for assistance.

PURPOSE

With this plan, ABC Inc. seeks to fulfill the following objectives:

- Provide a level of security and safety for employees in the event of a disaster.
- Minimize the operational risk and maximize the speed in setting up an alternate location.
- Minimize the spontaneous decisions that need to be made during a disaster.
- Ensure continuation of service to customers.
- Receive positive media coverage as a result of advanced planning.
- Enable timely communication to customers and vendors.
- Insurance claims can be made and received timely.
- Develop a goals approach for periodically testing the BCP plan.
- Create methodologies for effectively communicating the plan to employees.
- Creating a process to periodically revise and update the plan.
- Create a plan that will ensure ABC Inc.' survival by:
  - Ensuring Insurance coverage is adequate.
  - Ensuring everyone knows where to go and what to do in the event of an emergency.
  - Protecting shareholders/owners' interests.

STRATEGY

The strategy of the ABC, Inc. contingency plan is as follows:

- Ensure that all relevant computer software and databases are duplicated and stored in a secure off-site location for use in recovery.
- Provide alternate processing strategies to support essential business functions and maintain cash flow during a disaster recovery period.
- Publish and maintain this policy memorandum as a plan that can be used as a reference should a disaster actually occur.
- Identify responsibility to restore voice communications in the event of a loss of telephone service.
- Provide for plan maintenance and systems changes.

RISK MANAGEMENT PROGRAM

Risk management programs outline tasks and responsibilities necessary to support ant maintain an effective ongoing disaster recovery and business continuation plan, before a localized disaster occurs.

Simplified business continuity plan (continued)

Responsibility	Action
Technologies Manager	Ensure that all relevant files and databases are consistently backed up in accordance with the processing frequency indicated on application data sheets.
Senior Operator	Rotate magnetic tapes representing databases and data sets based on existing daily, weekly, and monthly schedules to the off-site location.
Operations Manager	Store source programs, compiled programs, operating systems, data communication, and related system software at the off-site location…

[The Risk Management Program section should include subsections with text or tables that show the results of four worksheets: (a) risk assessment, (b) risk mitigation strategies, (c) business impact assessment, and (d) early warning systems.]

CRISIS RESPONSE PROGRAM

An emergency response plan identifies required tasks and responsibilities that must be addressed at the time a specific disaster occurs or are needed to establish temporary operations and data processing capability at another location. It contains actions assigned to specific individuals as well as to an emergency response team who may work individually or collectively at the discretion of the information systems manager.

Responsibility	Action
Manager on Duty	Recognize and declare the emergency and notify proper authorities, such as the police, fire, and utility departments, based on the nature of the disaster, and the Emergency Response Team.
Emergency Response Team	Determine whether the business continuation plan is activated and under which scenario. Notify the emergency response team leader …

[The Crisis Response Program section should include subsections with text or tables that show the results of two worksheets: (e) initial responses, (f) notifications list, (and (g) business continuity strategies (critical functions for recovery).]

Appendix A	Building Evacuation Plan
Appendix B	Other appendices …

Narrative With Integrated Data

One way to write your plan is to integrate most or all your information into a narrative document. The worksheets that issue from the exercises present data that can be inserted into a plan as tables to create sections within your narrative document with headings like risk assessment, risk mitigation strategies, early warning system, and business continuity. This approach would probably contain just one appendix: the emergency contacts list.

Policy Overview With Appendices

An easier and quicker way to write a BCP is by appending your completed worksheets to a short, cover policy document that explains the objectives and methodology of the plan, as illustrated in Figure 9.2. This format lends itself to easy, continuous updates of sections without having to rewrite the full report. Organized this way, it is also easier for your people to use sections relevant to them during an emergency.

The recommended sections for a plan are executive summary, policy, scope, purpose, strategy, risk management program overview, and emergency response overview. Descriptions of these sections are given below.

Executive summary should introduce the reader to the plan's overall purpose, objectives, and general findings. With a few edits, our suggested BCP example's executive summary may be generic enough for your use.

Policy states what the objectives of a BCP are: to provide an organized response to an isolated disaster that would endanger personnel safety or render communications, computers, or facilities inoperable or inaccessible; and to prevent a significant deterioration in either cash flow or our ability to service customer

Figure 9.2: Suggested BCP organization

orders during a stabilization period.

Scope is the first step in developing your plan. With some exceptions, it's not necessary for the plan to include separate strategies to suit specific disaster scenarios.

An easier approach is to prepare just for a worst-case scenario, brought on by any disaster; a situation in which your people are facing or have experienced harm, and the primary workplace has been destroyed or rendered unusable.

In a worst-case scenario all the features of a plan can be invoked fully or selectively; but a fundamentally "light" plan can't be scaled up in a crunch.

Purpose of your BCP is to protect your business from unexpected disruptions through early warnings, and to mitigate disruptions that can't be avoided through preconceived strategies.

The central theme of your plan should be to minimize operational downtime and systems failures while insuring the maximum amount of organizational stability during the recovery period after a disaster.

Strategy of a contingency plan is as follows:

- Provide the safest environment possible for your workforce, consistent with a risk-based assessment
- Provide alternate, manual processing strategies to support key business functions and maintain market share during a stabilization period
- Ensure that all relevant electronic databases are duplicated and stored in a secure off-site location for use in recovery (but do not rely only on cloud-based systems as you cannot count on the Internet during a crisis)
- Publish an organized plan, a BCP, that can be used as a reference should a disaster actually occur
- Adjust to personnel turnover and environmental and systems changes

Risk management program section assesses the potential threats, finds ways to mitigate the threats to an acceptable level, and identifies indicators of incipient crises to trigger responses. It is also when organizations research and apply lessons learned from its own experiences and from others. Finally, it assigns direct responsibility for specific actions to existing position descriptions.

"In a worst-case scenario all the features of a plan can be invoked fully or selectively; but a fundamentally 'light' plan can't be scaled up in a crunch."

In short, risk management encompasses those activities that prepare the company for a crisis and keeps it prepared by providing for periodic testing and applying lessons learned. The results of Chapter 5 exercises using the following forms can be appended to the BCP and referenced in this section:

- Risk assessment (Appendix A.3 on page 158)
- Risk mitigation strategies (Appendix A.4 on page 159)
- Early warning system (Appendix A.5 on page 160)

Crisis response program section contains the tools for responding to crises that cannot be averted.

Although a thorough analysis of operating systems will have categorized systems into critical and non-critical functions, the efficacy of a crisis response program's logistical preparations and continuity strategies become truly evident at the time of an actual disaster or a *business interruption* test (page 147). It also depends on the nature of the disaster, the point in its development when the disaster is sensed and fronted, and the length of disruption.

A sound plan will have inventoried all the functions—the

relatively few daily routines that must be performed to keep products moving and keep the company solvent—through business continuity surveys and the resulting strategies and response worksheets. This section should reference the following four worksheets from Chapters 6 and 7 as appendices to the plan:

- Business continuity strategies (Appendix A.6 on page 161)
- Emergency contacts list (Appendix A.7 on page 162)
- Crisis response program (Appendix A.8 on page 164)
- Crisis grab kit list (Appendix A.9 on page 165)

Depending on your circumstances, your organization may also include other appendices not covered in this book, such as an evacuations plan tab, as illustrated in Figure 9.2.

A crisis response program identifies clearly the individuals who will execute the plan by names or, preferably, by functional titles. The assignments should be linked and accountable to specific actions in the plan.

Assignments by title are particularly important in a company with significant personnel turnover so that crisis response duties attached to a title carry on regardless of what person is filling the position temporarily or as a permanent assignment. Figure 7.1 on page 110 illustrates our way to assign people by title to response functions.

Administration

Depending on the size of your entity, you may have more than one team to organize. Teams should be comprised of representatives with varying skills from all departments. You can also arrange to include vendors and affiliated companies you depend on.

Organizations with many people should establish multiple teams, each with a designated leader. The primary responsibilities for each team will be to activate a portion of the BCP, log their recovery events, and report recovery status.

Once established, all team members should be trained and periodically retrained in their responsibilities. Training sessions should include a review of each team's responsibilities, the team's membership, an overview of the full emergency action plan, and a review of the sections relevant to each team. The following two teams show a suggested division of labor for a crisis.

Crisis Management Team

The purpose and responsibility of this team is to coordinate all activities during the recovery period. The general areas of responsibility may include implementing administrative controls and communicating the recovery status to senior management. Among these responsibilities are:

- Disaster declaration
- Documentation of recovery activities
- Senior management liaison
- Plan execution
- Staff assignments
- Activation of recovery teams
- Communication with system users
- Financial and policy decisions
- Vendor interface
- Media interface
- Preparation of recovery site and command center
- Establishment of telecommunications network
- Coordination of transportation
- Implement alternative processing procedures
- Security at an alternate site
- Relocation of equipment, personnel, supplies to alternate site
- Obtaining system and other documentation

Reconstruction Team

The purpose and responsibility of this team is to restore the primary facility back to full operation as soon as possible. Following are the more obvious functions that need to be addressed at the break of a crisis:

- Damage assessment
- Security
- Equipment salvage
- Insurance claims
- Equipment purchase and installation
- Site planning
- Site construction
- Vendor interface
- Restoration of primary site

Each of the two teams are slated to perform many functions. A very small company may have only one team performing all the functions. On the other hand, companies with many people or facilities could organize more teams than these two.

■   ■   ■

A completed plan will give you a measure of peace, but you will have one more task to perform to complete your BCP: to test it while your systems are in order to assure that you will not be caught with a faulty plan in a crisis.

10

PARACHUTE GEAR CHECKS

The road to wisdom? Well, it's plain and
simple to express: Err and err and err
again but less and less and less.

— Piet Hein

PARACHUTISTS ALWAYS CHECK and test their rigs before they go operational. Inspections and testing should be included as part of the business continuity plan. You need to test your plan in detail and evaluate it regularly—at least once a year—before a crisis happens.

There are many good reasons for testing periodically. For instance, environmental changes will occur as your organization grows, new equipment is purchased and new policies and procedures are developed. And time will erode the staff's memory and leave critical parts of the plan forgotten.

Without upkeep, inevitable changes over time will render the best laid plan a useless rag just when you need to arrest your fall.

The benefits of testing are many and include the following:

- Verifying the compatibility of the off-site recovery location
- Ensuring the adequacy of action plans
- Identifying deficiencies in your existing procedures
- Training of recovery teams, managers and staff
- Demonstrating the ability of your company to recover
- Providing a method for maintaining and updating your plan

Training to support critical skills that may be needed during a disaster is an important part of the testing process. These special skills include first aid, fire extinguishing, evacuation procedures, protection of assets and proprietary information, emergency communication methods, and shutdown procedures for equipment, electricity, water and gas.

TYPES OF TESTS

Some very standard ways to test your systems range from the simple checklist to assure that everything is in place (but it will not tell you if everything is functioning), to a full-blown test where you literally cause a deliberate system shutdown to force your crew to practice a real recovery. They are discussed below.

Checklist testing determines whether adequate supplies are stored at the alternate location, telephone number listings are current, adequate forms are available, and that continuity plans and operations manuals are available.

Under this testing scenario the recovery team reviews the plan and identifies key elements that should be up-to-date and available. A checklist test ensures that each department is in compliance with the requirements of the business continuity plan. It is simple, requires minimal human resources and does not interrupt anything.

Non-business interruption testing will simulate a disaster without interrupting normal business processes. A disaster test plan of this type should evaluate and rate the following things:

- Purpose of the test
- Objectives
- Timing, scheduling, and duration of the test
- Participants and their assignments
- Constraints and assumptions
- Test steps

This test can include notification procedures, emergency operating procedures and the off-site recovery center. Hardware, software, recovery personnel, telecommunications, supplies, forms, all needed documentation, off-site records storage, transportation, and utilities should be tested adequately during a non-business interruption scenario.

It may not be practical or economically feasible to perform tasks like travel or moving equipment during a simulated test. So a combination of the checklist test and the non-business interruption test may be a practical way for initial tests so required modifications can be identified before testing extensively.

Parallel testing can be performed in tandem with the checklist test or non-business interruption test. Under this scenario, historical transactions can be processed against the preceding day's backup at the alternate processing location. All reports normally produced at the alternate location for the current business day should agree with those reports produced at your normal business location.

Business interruption testing implements the total business continuity plan. This test is costly and could disrupt your normal business operations, so proceed with caution!

Adequate time must be allotted for this test. The initial test should not be performed during critical times of the data processing cycle, for example, fiscal year end processing.

The length of the test should be based on how quickly your needs are to recover in a disaster situation, and can be used to determine where you need to improve the recovery process.

Numerous test scenarios could be planned to identify the type of disaster, the extent of damage, recovery capability, resource availability, backup availability, and the time and the duration of the test.

Your test should include the persons with recovery responsibilities, and the time designated for each to perform their activities. Initially, you may want to test only certain portions of the plan to identify the feasibility of each part prior to attempting a full test.

It may also be wise to perform a business interruption test after normal business hours or on a weekend to minimize disruption. Once you feel comfortable with the test results, an unannounced test should be done to emphasize preparedness.

FREQUENCY OF TESTS

Many regulatory agencies require that certain types of companies test their plan at least annually. It's in your best interest to test your plan at least once a year, if not more frequently, whether or not your company is required to by regulation.

A relatively new plan should be subjected to quarterly or semiannual tests. After the first year, a semiannual or annual test should be incorporated into your company's policies and procedures manual.

In planning tests, remember the range of crises that can affect you. Don't drill only for fires, earthquakes or hurricanes. You should test for such events as a labor strike, or a serious industrial accident, or a criminal attack and other threats, because different crises can invoke different responses and complications.

Your recovery teams should evaluate test results by logging events during the testing process that will later assist you in evaluating the results. Recovery teams also assess the test results and make modifications that will improve the process and trim valuable minutes.

When dealing with critical applications, every minute cut from the restoration process can translate into significant savings in money. Therefore, it is recommended that you measure the results *quantitatively*, to include—

- The time to perform various action items,
- The accuracy of each activity,
- The amount of work completed, and
- Management approval and sign-off

Once you conduct your first test of the plan by one or more of the tests described in this chapter you will have completed the project you set out to accomplish. Having tested the system successfully, you will then be able to get the company's leadership to approve and sign off on the plan.

But the process should not stop there. Continuity and disaster preparation plans can and will quickly become outdated and ineffective if they are not maintained regularly. The larger the organization, the truer this is.

Constant turnover of personnel and systems will require that you continue to update your plan, train your personnel and test the system regularly.

■ ■ ■

If you look back to Figure 2.1 on page 38, you will notice in the Risk Intelligence and Solutions Cycle that learning and auditing are an important part of the continuing process, whether the lessons learned result from contrived tests or actual crises.

The wise organization will put its business continuity plan to the "fire" regularly to assure that its personnel stay versed, that new systems are taken into account and tested, and that its strategies for dealing with critical functions remain viable.

A famous Scottish poet, Robert Burns, long ago quipped thus:

The best laid plans take 40 years to complete.

Centuries later, J. K. Rowling, wrote this line in her 2015 book, *Harry Potter and the Deathly Hollows*:

*I have been careless, and so have been
thwarted by luck and chance, those wreckers
of all but the best laid plans.*

Don't let your plan grow stale!

APPENDICES

This section contains the worksheets that help the reader gather, analyze and act on his or her company's information. The worksheets are various parachute parts needed to build a business continuity plan.

A P P E N D I X

PARACHUTE PARTS

THIS APPENDIX PROVIDES the worksheets in blank form. The worksheets in this book can be photocopied for individual use, but you may find it easier to download them from the publisher's website at www.quest-publishing.com.

The electronic versions of the exercise worksheets are in full U.S. letter-size (8.5"X11") to give users more space to work with. They are provided in thee formats: *rich text format* (.rtf), *Microsoft Word* document (.docx) and *portable document format* (.pdf). They can be opened in most any word processor or operating system for use or printing.

The following two downloadable forms are also available as *Microsoft Excel* spreadsheets that are programmed to perform the mathematical calculations for the user:

- BCP Project Plan

- Risk Assessment

The publisher will provide updated forms from time to time to incorporate corrections, new features recommended by readers, or other improvements as needed.

Appendix A.1: Business Continuity Project Plan

TASK	TASK NAME	DURATION	START	FINISH	ASSIGNED
1	**Initiate the BCM Project**				
2	Get management buy-in				
3	Identify the Plan Administrator				
4	Identify the Plan Creation Team				
5	Communicate the plan to others				
6	**Business Impact Assessment**				
7	Review current plans				
8	Establish an early warning system				
9	Audit the company's preparedness				
10	Conduct a threat assessment				
11	Conduct a vulnerability assessment				
12	Produce a cost-benefit analysis				
13	Identify critical business functions				
14	Write the BIA document				
15	**Business Continuity Plan**				
16	Position/educate plan contributors				
17	Develop continuity strategies				
18	Document continuity strategies				
19	Create a contact list				
20	Create prep. press releases				
21	Write the BCP document				
22	**Accountability & Compliance**				
23	Assign responsibilities to individuals				
24	Establish Emergency Response Team				
25	Establish Reconstruction Team				
26	Write "team assignments" memo				
27	**Test the Plan**				
28	Checklist test				
29	Prepare non-bus. int. test scenario				
30	Non-business interruption test				
31	Prepare parallel test scenario				
32	Parallel test				
33	Prepare bus. interruption test scenario				
34	Business interruption test				
35	Project pass/need improv. Report				
36	Correct issues				
37	Test again				
38	Write BCM program "ready" report				
39	**Institute Your BCM Program**				

Appendix A.2: Business Continuity Survey

Name: _____

Title: _____

Department: _____

This survey is to identify the absolutely critical functions that your section/department/company must perform within __ days in order to survive. Such functions contribute directly to the organization's bottom line and without which the organization's survival is questionable. Typically, such functions include production, client relations, cash flow operations, etc. Please complete the following sections in preparation/update of our company business continuity plan (BCP). Use the following scale to rate the "criticality" of functions as they affect your area.

CRITICALITY SCALE	Comments
1 = Most Critical	needed immediately; cannot function without it
2 = Highly Critical	cannot disrupt longer than ___ hours without risking the company
3 = Critical	cannot disrupt longer than ___ days without risking the company
4 = Secondary	disruption past ___ week(s) would hurt operations
5 = Non-critical	disruption would be an inconvenience but would not risk the company

Criticality of Functions

For all applicable, use the criticality scale to rate the functions that are in your purview in, and add any other function that is not listed and you believe is also critical:

☐	Billing (accounts receivable)	☐	Billing (accounts payable)
☐	Job scheduling	☐	Job execution
☐	Shipping	☐	Customer service
☐	Order processing	☐	Payroll
☐	Media relations	☐	Other: _____

Tasks Associated to Applicable Functions

List any tasks that **need** to be performed in support of the critical functions listed above. Also list any equipment, forms or communications devices needed to perform the tasks.

▷ _____

▷ _____

▷ _____

▷ _____

▷ _____

Business Continuity Survey (continued)

Existing Replacement Arrangements (to replace existing systems or equipment or supplies)

▷ _____

▷ _____

▷ _____

Essential Operating Procedures (needed to maintain an efficient workflow)

▷ _____

▷ _____

▷ _____

Equipment or Supplies for Off-Site Storage

▷ _____

▷ _____

▷ _____

Vital Records (those that are uniquely valuable to you in your purview)

▷ _____

▷ _____

▷ _____

Back-up Procedures (for servers, desktop/notebook computers in your purview)

▷ _____

▷ _____

▷ _____

Temporary Operating Procedures (in the event your office facility becomes unavailable)

▷ _____

▷ _____

▷ _____

▷ _____

▷ _____

▷ _____

Appendix A.3: Risk Assessment

Threat	Prob. X	Vulnerability		X	Consequence			= RISK
		Int. + Ext. = Sum			Business + Assets + People = Sum Functions /Prop.			

LEGEND:
Prob. = probability of occurring
Int. = internal resources
Ext. = external resources

Vulnerability Criteria:
1 Well mitigated (through assets, personnel, vendors and/or procedures)
2 Adequately mitigated (good but for minor weakness/issue)
3 Poorly mitigated or not mitigated (an important weakness remains)

Threat Probability Criteria:
1 Unlikely to occur
2 Could occur (moderate)
3 Likely to occur

Consequence Criteria:
1 No discernable impact on business, assets or people
2 Negative but surmountable effects on operations, assets or people
3 Potentially disrupts or paralyzes operations and hampers output

Ranges: 5 to 30 = low risk | 31 to 55 = moderate risk | 55 to 80 = high risk | 81+ = dangerous weakness

Appendix A.4: Risk Mitigation Strategies

Type of Risk	Action or Product	Source	Action by

Appendix A.5: Early Warning System

Risk Description	Source (what to monitor)	Signal (alarming event)	Immediate Response	Monitor

Appendix A.6: Business Continuity Strategies

Cr.	Function	Alternate Method

Cr. = criticality

Appendix A.7: Emergency Contacts

Building Crisis Center _____

Building Manager's Name/Telephone _____

Fire/Rescue Services _____

Miami-Dade Office of Emergency Mgt. _____

Local Police Departments

    City of Miami _____

    County Sheriff's Office _____

Bomb Disposal _____

Hazardous Materials/Telephone _____

Electric Company

    Contact _____

    In Case of Outage _____

Water Company

    In Case of Outage _____

Telephone Company

    Contact _____

    In Case of Outage _____

Internet Provider

    Contact _____

    Ordering, Billing, Other Services _____

Medical Facilities _____

    Address _____

    Telephone _____

Alternate Relocation Site _____

    Warm Site _____

    Telephone _____

Business Insurance Company _____

    Point of Contact _____

    Address _____

    Telephone _____

Emergency Contacts (continued)

Key Client 2 _____

    Name _____

    Address _____

    Telephone _____

Key Client 3 _____

    Name _____

    Address _____

    Telephone _____

Key Supplier 1 _____

    Name _____

    Address 1 _____

    Telephone _____

Key Supplier 2 _____

    Name _____

    Address _____

    Telephone _____

Media Contact 1 _____

    Name _____

    Point of Contact _____

    Address _____

    Telephone _____

Media Contact 2 _____

    Name _____

    Point of Contact _____

    Address _____

Media Contact 3 _____

    Name _____

    Point of Contact _____

    Address _____

    Telephone _____

Appendix A.8: Crisis Response Actions

Responsibility	Action

Appendix A.9: Crisis Grab Kit

Qty.	Item Description	Team/Purpose	Destination

B

RELATED INTERNET LINKS

The following Internet sites are listed in the alphabetical order of their sponsors:

Association of Threat Assessment Professionals (ATAP) provides its members with opportunities for education and professional recognition through certifications in the practice of assessing threats to persons and entities. ATAP is organized into chapters and holds periodic conferences. Website: *www.atapworldwide.org.*

BCMpedia is the "wiki" section for business continuity management and disaster recovery of the BCM Institute, a non-profit organization of BCM professionals that originated in Asia and is expanding to Europe and the Americas. Website: *www.bcmpedia.org.*

Business Continuity Institute (BCI) publishes information on standards and training opportunities for business continuity professionals. Website: *www.thebci.org.*

Casualty Actuarial Society (CAS) includes educational resources, research projects and presentations on the topic of enterprise risk management (ERM). One of the purposes of the organization is to advance the knowledge of actuarial science applied to general insurance, including property, casualty and similar risk exposures. Website: *www.casact.org.*

Centre for Analysis of Risk and Regulation (CARR) is an interdisciplinary research center focused on organizational and institutional settings for risk management and regulatory practices. Its publishing program includes a biannual magazine, discussion papers, books and special reports. Website: *www.lse.ac.uk.*

Continuity Forum provides information and support for disaster recovery, crises management, emergency planning, and security management with the aim of improving organizational resilience. Website: *www.continuityforum.org.*

Federal Emergency Management Agency (FEMA) dedicates a section of its website to business continuity planning. It provides information on creating plans for crisis communication, emergency response, implementation of a business continuity plan, testing, exercises and program improvement. Website: *www.ready. gov/business.*

Free Management Library is an online collection of articles about myriad business-related topics for personal, professional and organizational development. A part of the site is a section that is focused on crisis management. Website: *managementhelp.org/crisismanagement/.*

Global Association of Risk Professionals (GARP) is a globally recognized membership association for risk managers. Website: *www.garp.com.*

infoplease is a "wiki" type of website that dedicates a page to information about catastrophic natural and human-caused disasters. Although it is not all-inclusive, their lists of events are still a good reference source for disasters that have caused great losses of life and/or property, are of historical interest, or had unusual circumstances. Website: *www.infoplease.com/ipa/A0001437. html.*

Institute of Internal Auditors (IIA) is an international professional association focused on internal auditing, risk management, governance, internal control, information technology, and security. It issues books, periodicals, standards and guidance on various issues and provides training activities. Website: *www.theiia.org.*

Institute of Risk Management (IRM) is intended for risk management professionals and provides training, recognizes qualifications, sponsors events and issues publications. Website: *www.theirm.org.*

Insurance Information Institute (III) provides good descriptions of the various types of business insurance policies. Website: *www.iii.org/insurance-topics/business.*

Insurance Professional is for insurance professionals *and* insurance consumers. This site provides an exhaustive list of property and casualty insurance companies. Website: *www.einsuranceprofessional.com/inscomp.html.*

International Organization for Standardization (ISO) is an independent, non-governmental organization that groups international experts into teams that develop consensus-based voluntary international standards for myriad fields of work. The aim of the standards is to "support innovation and provide solutions to global challenges." It has established the "ISO 22301:2012 – Societal security – Business continuity management systems" standard for entities desiring or that are required to meet a recognized ISO approach. This standard specifies requirements for planning, establishing, implementing, operating, monitoring, reviewing, maintaining and continually improving a documented management system to protect against or mitigate disruptive incidents. Website: *www.iso.org.*

International Risk Governance Council (IRGC) is an independent organization whose purpose is to help understand and manage global risks that impact on human health and safety, the environment, the economy and society at large. Website: *www.ircg.org.*

McKinsey & Company is a leading consulting firm. Its website, www.mckinsey.com, dedicates a section titled "Working Papers on Risk" that is dedicated to risk issues. The section presents a series of white papers on McKinsey's best current thinking about risk and risk management. The papers represent a broad range of views intended to encourage discussion internally and externally. Website: *www.mckinsey.com/client_service/ risk/latest_thinking/working_papers_on_risk.*

National Center for Spectator Sports Safety and Security (NCS[4]) is a department of The University of Southern

Mississippi dedicated to research, training, education and outreach in support of sport safety and security. It promotes DHS/FEMA programs and its own academic research and instruction to issue professional certifications in sports security. Website: *https://ncs4. usm.edu.*

Open Compliance and Ethics Group (OCEG) is a nonprofit entity that helps organizations use OCEG's "Principled Performance®" by enhancing their corporate culture and integrating governance, risk management, and compliance processes. Website: *www.oceg.org.*

Reputation Institute is a leading consultancy providing companies with best practices in reputation management. Website: *www.reputationinstitute.com.*

RISCAuthority is funded by a group of United Kingdom insurers to represent them and to conduct research that identifies best practices about the protection of property and businesses. Website: *www.riscauthority. co.uk.*

Risk Management Society (RIMS) is a global not-for-profit organization representing more than 3,500 industrial, service, not-for-profit, charitable and government entities throughout the world. It is aimed at corporate risk management professionals. Website: *www.rims.org.*

SANS Institute is a private for-profit company that specializes in cybersecurity and information security. It provides a range of courses and certifications. Website: *www.sans.org.*

Social Science Research Network (SSRN)   is devoted to the worldwide dissemination of social science research and is composed of a number of specialized research networks in each of the social sciences including corporate governance, law, management, economics, and other topics. Website: *www.ssrn.com.*

APPENDIX

GLOSSARY

5G is the fifth generation (newest and fastest) technology standard for broadband cellular networks.

A is denoted as "a" and is one of three sub variables that sum to the value of "Consequence" or "C" in the T * (i + e) * (f + a + p) = R, or T * V * C = R risk assessment equation.

ASAP acronym for "as soon as possible."

BCM Business Continuity Management, and encompasses the range of activities from planning for potentially crippling crises, mitigating the threats, testing the plan, and learning from testing or actual critical events.

BCP Business Continuity Plan, the written product of your research for creating a RISC/business continuity management program.

BIA Business Impact Assessment, which consolidates operational information from an organization's different units or departments to identify and rank the critical functions that must be performed manually or otherwise in the event of a crisis.

BOP   Business Owner's Policy, and it normally includes policies that include comprehensive coverage for most or all insurance contingencies normally associated with operating a business. Also referred to as all-in-one, the aggregated coverage is normally cheaper than buying the parts individually.

C   is the "Consequence" variable, denoted as "C" in our $T * V * C = R$ equation. C is comprised of the sum of the impact on three sub variables: business function (f) + assets (a) + people (p).

CBA   Cost-Benefit Analysis, is a calculation of costs and benefits, usually in table form, to facilitate the comparison of various options as solutions to a stated problem. Comparisons are usually measured in monetary terms.

CEO   Chief Executive Officer.

CIO   Chief Information Officer.

CM   Crisis Management, the part of the RISC cycle that includes responding to and resolving hypothetical or actual crises, guided by an existing business continuity plan.

Cloud   computing systems, particularly for data storage and backups, available to users through the Internet.

CMT   Crisis Management Team, is the team of individuals identified by the leadership to train together to test the organization's business continuity plan for flaws or weaknesses, and to respond in concert to mitigate and resolve actual crises.

CRO   Chief Risk Officer

E   is denoted as "e" and is one of two sub variables that sum to the value of "Vulnerability" or "V" in the T * (i + e) * (f + a + p) = R, or T * V * C = R risk assessment equation.

EDI   Electronic Data Interchange, is a protocol for securely exchanging business documents with partners, such as placing or receiving orders electronically.

EMC   Emergency Management Committee, has the same functions as a CMT but tends to be more formalized, larger, and authorized by top management or a board to represent the broader organization.

EWS   Early Warning System, is a preconceived set of indicators, like an activated smoke alarm or a key officer's bad medical report, that presumably foretell the potential for a crisis or the beginnings of one.

F   is denoted as "f" and is one of three sub variables that sum to the value of "Consequence" or "C" in the T * (i + e) * (f + a + p) = R, or T * V * C = R risk assessment eqution.

I   is denoted as "i" and is one of two sub variables that sum to the value of "Vulnerability" or "V" in the T * (i + e) * (f + a + p) = R, or T * V * C = R risk assessment equation.

LLC   Limited Liability Company, ia a legal business structure in the U.S. that provides limited liability for its owners.

MIS   Management Information System, refers to the mechanisms and processes used to store, manipulate, organize and retrieve an organization's data and information.

OSHA   Occupational Safety and Health Administration.

P   is denoted as "p" and is one of three sub variables that sum to the value of "Consequence" or "C" in the T * (i + e) * (f + a + p) = R, or T * V * C = R risk assessment equation.

PII   Personally Identifiable Information, is any financial, health or educational data about an individual that can be used to impersonate the individual (identity theft) or commit other forms of fraud.

PR   Public Relations, are those activities that an organization engages in to engender good-will and communications channels with media outlets to promote the organization's image and community standing.

R   is the "Risk" variable, denoted as "R" in our T * V * C = R equation.

RISC   Risk Intelligence and Solutions Cycle™, is the model that describes all the interrelated activities that occur in business continuity and risk and crisis management. It is similar to business continuity management but it is more extensive in that it also deals with crises that are less than potentially crippling or fatal to an organization, but still a crisis.

RM   Risk Management, is the preventive aspect of the RISC cycle that includes the preparation for potential crises through learning, detection, and public relations. It includes the assessments, mitigation strategies and continuity strategies that form a business continuity plan.

RTO   Recovery Time Objective, is the stated time span within which specified systems need to be restored to keep the organization functioning and eventually return it to normalcy. It is usually stated in terms of hours or days.

SaaS   Software as a Service; is a free or fee-based software service that is delivered and used under licence through the Internet rather than being installed and run locally on a computing device.

SWAT   Special Weapons and Tactics, are teams of law enforcement officers specially trained for dangerous tactical missions, such as hostage rescue, barricaded subjects, prison uprisings, active shooters or dangerous raids.

SWOT   Strengths / Weaknesses / Opportunities / Threats, is a popular business analysis tool for assessing one's own business versus competitors to identify competitive advantages, marketing opportunies, threats to the organization, and recognize, overcome or minimize the business' disadvantages and weaknesses.

T   is the "Threat" variable, denoted as a "T" in our

T * (i + e) * (f + a + p) = R, or T * V * C = R risk assessment equation.

UPS   Uninterrupted Power Supply, is an always-ready, stand-by source of power attached to critical equipment with volatile memory, such as computerized equipment.

V   is the "Vulnerability" variable, denoted as "V" in our T * V * C = R equation. V is comprised of the sum of two variables to meet a threat: the adequacy of internal resources (i), and the dependability on external resources (e).

VOIP   Voice Over Internet Protocol, telephone service that transmits digitized voice through Internet channels rather than through a traditional telephone network.

WIP   work-in-progress.

Bibliography

Barr, James G. 2002. *Conducting a Business Impact Analysis*. Faulkner Information Services. www.amazon.com (download).

Caponigro, Jeffrey R. 1998. *The Crisis Counselor: The Executive's Guide to Avoiding, Managing and Thriving on Crisis That Occur in all Businesses*. Barker Business Books.

FEMA and American Red Cross. 1993. *Emergency Management Guide for Business & Industry*.

FEMA. 2019. *Business Process Analysis and Business Impact Analysis User Guide*.

Franklin, Barbara. 2004. "BCP Introduction and Logistics Workshop Program." Session syllabus for the Coral Gables Chamber of Commerce BCP workshop, supplied to the author by Barbara Franklin.

Gelnovatch, Bruce. 2003. "Business Continuity Planning." White paper supplied to the author by Bruce Gelnovatch.

Myers, Kenneth N. 1999. *Manager's Guide to Contingency Planning for Disasters: Protecting Vital Facilities and Critical Operations*. New York: Wiley & Sons, 2nd Ed.

National Research Council. 2010. *Review of the Department of Homeland Security's Approach to Risk Analysis*. Washington, D.C.: The National Academies Press. https://doi.org/10.17226/12972.

New York State. Insurance Department and Empire State Development. 2012. *Property Casualty Insurance: A Small Business Guide*. Download from https://www.dfs.ny.gov/consumers/small_businesses/prop_casualty_guide.

Osterman Research, Inc. 2017. *Second Annual State of Ransomware Report: US Survey Results*. July 2017. Download from https://assets.toolbox.com/research/osterman-research-second-annual-state-of-ransomware-report-us-survey-results-53163.

Pinon, Joseph R. 2010. "Response to a Crisis of Pandemic Proportions." White paper supplied to the author by Joseph Pinon.

U.S. Department of Health and Human Services. National Institutes of Health. 2004. *Cost-Benefit Analysis Guide for NIH IT Projects*. Download from https://www.scribd.com/document/189713633/Nih-Guidelines.

Wisconsin State. Office of the Commissioner of Insurance. *Consumers' Guide to Insurance for Small Business Owners*. 2019. Download from https://oci.wi.gov/Documents/Consumers/PI-085.pdf.

Index

CPSIA information can be obtained
at www.ICGtesting.com
Printed in the USA
LVHW051047070221
678582LV00016B/488